T0148303

INSTRUCTIONAL
TECHNOLOGY TOOLS

{ A PROFESSIONAL
DEVELOPMENT PLAN

L. Robert Furman, EdD

iUniverse, Inc.
Bloomington

iUniverse books may be ordered through booksellers or by contacting:

iUniverse
1663 Liberty Drive
Bloomington, IN 47403
www.iuniverse.com
1-800-Authors (1-800-288-4677)

ISBN: 978-1-4697-8930-9 (sc)
ISBN: 978-1-4697-8931-6 (e)

Library of Congress Control Number: 2012903744

Printed in the United States of America

iUniverse rev. date: 3/12/2012

E-Tool – A small, effective, website or application that could assist any school administrators or teachers to better educate their students, ease their workload, or enhance their school program.

Contents

Dedication

This publication is dedicated to Bob, Rosalie, Tiffeni, Luka, and Kyle Furman. They are my rock and my strength. When you have parents, a wife, and two beautiful children, as I do, you want to find ways to get your job done faster and smarter just so you can get home and be with the ones you love.

Preface

It is no longer appropriate to say technology "will" change the way we do things in the future. The future is here. The future is now, and technology *is* changing the way we do things. Many of us remember when we first heard of all these technological innovations, and we were told, "Someday this will change the way we work, play, and communicate." Now, with so much amazing technology available to us, we may feel like we are taking it for granted. Sometimes we may not be effectively using the amazing technology that we have available to us because we are always waiting for "someday."

This book is a professional development model that will give teachers and administrators working knowledge of specific technology e-tools and examples of how to incorporate these e-tools into their instructional plans. The mini-applications and websites discussed in the following pages are the very same items that we were told would change our future when we heard of them twenty years ago.

After sixteen years of teaching in and managing an elementary school, I have realized that as educators, we are always trying to find ways to enhance our classrooms, manage time, organize ourselves, and save money. The technology described in this book will do just that.

Acknowledgments

I would like to extend my sincere thanks to the following people, without whom this book could not have been written.

To Jeanine Gregory, the South Park administration, and the school board, I give my thanks for allowing me released time. This enabled me to share technological tools with not only our community stakeholders, but also to present E-Tools to other elementary principals at the National Association of Elementary School Principals' annual convention, the International Society for Technology in Education, and other national educational events.

To Lindsay, who worked tirelessly to help me create the wonderful tutorials found in this book.

To those principals who have taken their precious time to give me feedback on the use and value of the E-Tools included in this manuscript.

To Mom and Dad, for their constant and ever-present support. You have taught me that nothing is impossible.

To Tiff, Luka, and Kyle, for their inspiration. You are my rock.

Glossary of Terms

In the world of education, it is common to get confused by all the technology terminology. Every educator has had the experience of sitting around a table with a few non-educators who stare in confusion when the educational jargon is being tossed about. Even among educators, terms may differ from state to state. The same thing happens when technology specialists try to communicate with non-technology professionals. Below is a glossary of terms and abbreviations used in this publication. These definitions have been created by the author to avoid confusion.

E-Tool	A small, effective website or application that could assist any school administrators or teachers to better educate their students, ease their workload, or enhance their school program.
Instructional E-Tool	A technology tool that could enhance learning in the classroom. These E-Tools are mainly used for instructional purposes.
Management E-Tool	A technology tool that is beneficial for managing workflow. These E-Tools assist in doing research, collaborating on projects, enhancing communication, or simply saving time. Management E-Tools should be used by both administrators and teachers. Some management E-Tools may be considered instructional E-Tools as well.
Electronic Professional Development (E-ProDev)	E-ProDev is a system that allows teachers to go through a professional development day independently, accessing the information from any location that has a computer and an Internet connection. Among administrators, E-ProDev days may be used in place of in-service days.
Tutorial	A tutorial is a step-by-step instruction on how to use or how to create a project using one of the E-Tools. After completing a tutorial, a teacher should have working knowledge of how to use the E-Tool.

Instructional Technology Tools

As a principal in a typical middle-class elementary school, I am sure that when I bring up the subject of technology in the classroom, I hear the same concerns from teachers that many other school administrators hear. I hear the same concerns every time I send out the agenda for the next professional development day and the word "technology" is somewhere on that agenda. When administrators ask teachers to use technology, we often hear the following questions:

Why do we have to use this technology?

When are we going to have the time to learn how to use this new software?

It will take me twice as long to use the technology because I have to teach the students how to use it before I assign the project that uses the technology. Where is the time?

Technology never works in our school. Will this be available to us in the classroom when we want to use it, or will it be blocked?

Is our network strong enough to handle thirty students on the same web page at the same time?

Do these questions sound familiar? This manual will give your district's professional development presenter the answers to all of these difficult questions that teachers ask. These are the common obstacles that administrators have to overcome when presenting a professional development day that features technology. But there is hope.

Preparing an effective professional development day can be compared to what our teachers do when they prepare effective lessons in their classrooms. Our professional development days have to be engaging, with good pacing and solid outcomes. They have to be planned to accommodate all different types of learners and include an exciting, motivational beginning known as an anticipatory set that will grab our listeners from the beginning. We, as administrators, have to model the same quality of instruction that we expect from our teachers.

This book is designed to give the administrator all the tools necessary to conduct fulfilling and meaningful professional development days, in-house or electronically, revolving around the topic of technology. It will give you the ability to address those difficult questions the teachers have been asking. This publication also includes:

Professional development lesson plans

Tutorials for teachers and students

Sample sites where examples of each E-Tool are available for you to share

Addresses to obtain the E-Tools

As an administrator, you are the instructional leader. Administrators must take that title to heart and feel the power of that title to the core. As instructional leaders, we must be the models for excellent teaching. Opportunities to shine and model superior teaching lie in well-structured professional development days. We can win the hearts of our staff with one good, meaningful lesson. If we want the staff to use the E-Tools that we share with them, then we need to model those tools. If we want our schools to be on the cutting edge of instructional technology, then we must be willing to share the use of technology in our daily work.

Walden University, an online university, did a wonderful study on myths involving technology and education (Grunwald and Associates). Three of the myths are worth repeating here because they drive home the realization that some teachers and administrators are not all on the same page when it comes to technology.

Myth: Given that students today are already comfortable with technology, teachers' use of technology is less important to student learning.

The Walden study has shown that this statement simply is not true. Students perceive their teachers differently when a teacher uses technology versus when a teacher uses more traditional methods. The Walden study proved that technology has a positive effect on:

- Student behaviors
- Class attendance
- Focus and task completion
- Student achievement
- Dropout rate reduction
- Accommodation of high-needs students

Myth: Teachers and administrators have shared understandings about classroom technology and twenty-first-century skills.

This statement was sadly proven false as well. Teachers and administrators, according to this study, do not agree on technology and its usage. Administrators have a stronger desire to use technology than teachers do. One very important revelation was that administrators have a skewed belief that their teachers have more background in and knowledge about current technological skills and tools than teachers really do.

Myth: Teachers feel well prepared from their initial prep programs to effectively incorporate technology into instruction.

According to the Walden study, teachers who have been certified since 2000 generally do not feel well prepared in how to use technology in their classes. Teachers reported that continual professional development in technology increases their comfort with using technology in their instruction.

This manual will not only give you the tools necessary to hold positive, effective professional development days using technology, but will also give you many "techie tidbits" that you and your staff can use to save time, organize, collaborate, and so much more.

Money is often the magic word when it comes to using and sharing technology. Sadly, education has a tendency to get less and less money from the people who make the budget decisions. Being careful with your spending is the key to building a quality program. Every techie tidbit in this book, as of the time of printing, is free. *Free* is defined differently by each site, but overall, these techie tidbits can be used without charge as described in this book. Some sites have fee-based services that would be over and above what a free registration would allow, such as space to save more than one project, larger file sizes, more edit options, etc. There is no need to purchase any of these add-ons to get the benefit of these programs. However, if you do find one that you use a service more than most and/or you find a favorite, consider exploring the added benefits of a paid subscription.

Online Resource

As you go through this publication, visit http://www.furmanr.com. You will find examples of all of the E-Tools as well as a forum section where your faculty can upload their projects and responses. This will prove extremely valuable if you choose to engage in an Electronic Professional Development day (E-ProDev day). If you would like to have your own personal group where you can keep your faculty's responses private, please contact the author at L.R.Furman@gmail.com. Please feel free to leave comments about the applications or websites found in this book and to add a review of your own about how you used the applications or site. Also under the forums section, you may add a new E-Tool you may have found useful. The website that was used to create this online collaboration and review environment is one of the many E-Tools in this book. See, they do work!

Now let's attack those bothersome questions.

Typical Questions/ Concerns from Teachers

The teacher questions I listed previously are not the only ones we hear, but they are typically the basis of dispute when it comes to using technology. Below are some suggested responses to those questions/concerns.

Why do we have to use this technology?

There has been a research explosion when it comes to the benefits of technology in education. However, the best answers for the question *why* is more practical. Teachers get tired of hearing overquoted statistics and studies that have been controlled in a college lab setting. Teachers appreciate honest, logical answers to which they can relate on a practitioner level.

We need to use technology because the students we are teaching in today's classrooms were born and raised with technology. They expect to be taught using the devices of their generation. Think of it like this: we would not be expected to teach using an abacus and vinyl records. To our ears, those tools sound ridiculous because our generation was raised with CDs and calculators. We do not even think of the older generation of technology. Technology such as iPads and cell phones are normal tools for kids today, and we appear old-fashioned and out-of-date when we do not use what they have been using since birth.

When are we going to have the time to learn how to use this new software?

Educators have to think about technology in the same way they think about getting a new edition of a curriculum. First, administrators must give teachers time to get acquainted with the material. Then teachers should pilot various materials, using the materials without a heavy emphasis on grading or testing. Finally, teachers should choose the material that works best for them and their students and integrate it into their rotation of resources that they find to be useful.

It is the principal's responsibility to budget time for the staff to go through all of these steps.

Giving teachers time to create during a professional development day is essential. We will be discussing exactly how to go about allocating that necessary time in the following chapters. Administrators need to set the groundwork for introducing these new concepts.

A common misconception about professional development is that every minute of every hour in the professional development day must be devoted to continual, direct instruction. The principal must be in front of the staff, sharing, showing, and lecturing to them, for the day to be viewed as worthwhile time for the staff.

This is simply not true. As in any good lesson, there needs to be time for guided practice and exploration. Your staff needs time to be creative. They need time to explore the technology that you are sharing. It is also very important to give them clearly defined outcomes to demonstrate when they return from their own exploratory time. This will be further discussed in the chapter titled "Professional Development Plans."

It will take me twice as long to use the technology because I have to teach the students how to use it before I assign the project that uses the technology. Where is the time?

This is another misconception. We have to remember that the students are native to technology. They will pick up these programs faster than the average staff member. This book contains clear and commonsense tutorials on each of the E-Tools for both the teacher and the students. Many of these programs can be learned in twenty minutes or less, and a simple project completed within another twenty minutes. Teachers have been able to share a techie tidbit with examples, explain to the class how to create a project using the tutorial sheets, and guide students through the completion of a self-directed project within a standard forty-minute class period. The end result makes the extra time worthwhile.

Technology never works in our school. Will this be available to us in the classroom when we want to use it, or will it be blocked? Is our network strong enough to handle thirty students on the same web page at the same time?

These issues come up in every discussion dealing with technology. They are also very fair questions. Having been on the teacher side of the professional development table, I understand how incredibly upsetting it is to have a four-hour discussion and training on something technological, and then get back to the classroom to find the site blocked, or to have Internet access go down because every teacher is trying to get on the same website at the same time.

These are real issues and must be dealt with *before* you have any professional development days that deal with technology. Again, think of the professional development day as your opportunity to be the teacher. Imagine that someone was observing you teach in your classroom. You had a wonderful lesson prepared, but when your students turned on their computers, everything was blocked and frozen. The observer would not think this was a well-prepared lesson, and would assume some issues had not been addressed before the live lesson began.

With this example in mind, here are some steps to take a few days before you plan on having your professional development event.

1. Send a list of all the websites you will be using during your lesson to your instructional technology (IT) director at least two weeks before the scheduled date. Request that he/she check and unblock any sites that you have on the list. This may take some discussion to convince your IT director of the validity of the sites. Your position in this discussion could simply be that these sites are educator-tested and educator-approved. Send the IT director documentation from the websites that supports their worth to educators.

2. Check the websites one week before scheduled date to make sure they are working properly and that you can access them via your school computer.

3. Go through the tutorials that you will be using to make sure everything is logical and is still functional on each website.

4. Review the day's events with your IT director and make sure he/she understands the draw on the network that will happen when participants are using several computers at the same time. This issue was more of a concern several years ago, but schools that still have limited broadband connections may want to confirm that using multiple computers at the same time will not put too much stress on the network.

These steps will ensure a successful lesson. When the question comes up from your staff, you will be able to give a definite, honest response: "No, the site will not be blocked for you or your students, and yes, our system is strong."

Electronic Professional Development Days

Electronic Professional Development (E-ProDev) days have become a new and enticing concept for many school districts, especially those that deal with snow days. An E-ProDev day is a typical in-service, but performed online by the teachers, possibly even from home. The tutorials, lesson, and project are all given to the staff ahead of time. The teachers must go through the tutorial on their own, review the lesson, answer any questions that are in the lesson, and complete a project using the assigned technology.

Everything needed to hold an E-ProDev day can be found at http://www.furmanr.com. You may also have your staff turn in their projects to the community forum on the site. One of the E-Tools described in a later chapter is also a verification survey, in which the teachers must validate that they did everything as per the instructions. Once you return to school, you can review the verifications and check all of the projects.

The advantage of this for those in snowbelts, where days off from school can occur rather randomly, is that if you prepare these lessons and hand them out to the teachers in advance, you can count a snow day as a professional development day and not have to make it up per se. Just send out a notice as part of your snow-day announcement that it is also an E-ProDev day. Your staff will know to complete one of the several assignments you have made prior to snow season.

Professional Development Plans

Professional development is not only necessary for faculty and staff, but also essential for the school administrator. Professional development is critical for any leader to continue providing quality service for the organization. It gives the leader an opportunity to expand his or her skills beyond initial training and to acquire additional knowledge that will benefit the organization. A leader must also provide the model for lifelong learning. Furthermore, professional development should be linked to the actual practice of the profession; the effects of any training should be evident to one's colleagues. The effectiveness of an organization depends largely on the quality of its leader.

In many school districts, the planning of a professional development day rests solely on the shoulders of the administrators. Complaints from teachers about the day usually fall into the category of the use of time:

The professional development lesson was not something I could ever use in my classroom.

The professional development days are not a good use of my time.

I need time to be creative and work on enhancing my own lessons.

I already have too many initiatives, and I can never get a good, solid grasp on any one topic throughout the school year.

Knowing that you may get these responses is valuable as long as you have the autonomy to plan accordingly. Yes, we do want the material to be worthwhile and practical. Yes, we want the professional day to be valued, and we want the teachers to be as creative as possible and always enhancing their lessons. We want the teachers to feel that the initiative we are sharing is worth the time spent to master its functions. The model in this book takes into consideration all of these common concerns and helps the administrator or facilitator to respond to the staff.

The model presented in the following lesson plans can be arranged to fit the individual needs of the building or district. The model is broken down into suggested time segments and is easily adjustable for such things as lunch, prep times, scheduled breaks, and so on. The first agenda below is an example of a daylong staff development day. The second agenda is an example of a half-day plan. The third example is an example of an E-ProDev day. The E-ProDev day can be made a half-day or full-day session by adjusting the times.

It is recommended that technology be a focus throughout the school year and that administrators use multiple E-Tools from this publication to create meaningful, year-long, technology-focused professional development days. The second model is an example of how a year-long theme of technology can be established. The agendas give a short description for each period of time. In the reproducible appendix, there are blank agendas you can customize to meet your needs.

Each section also has presentation suggestions. The list of materials for each of the plans is similar and fortunately minimal. The materials needed are as follows:

Tutorial(s) from this book

3x5 cards (4 per person)

Marker

Video projection unit

Computer attached to the projection unit

Internet access

URL of the E-Tool and URL of your example (examples can be found at http://www. furmanr.com)

Full-day (8 Hour) Plan

Anticipatory Set (20–30 min.)

Preview the new instructional E-Tool and use an example from this book. Have teachers brainstorm ways to use the E-Tool in their classrooms. Share with the group. This is your opportunity to grab the attention of your audience and get them excited about using this technology.

Procedures (45–60 min.)

Using the tutorial provided, model each step of the process for creating a new project. This is the heart of your lesson, so you want to be sure that it's creative and motivational. Pause for questions and give a thorough explanation of each step of the process.

Guided Practice (20–30 min.)

The guided practice portion of your lesson may take on a different look depending on your situation. If you are teaching in a lab setting or have access to a wireless environment, this is a great opportunity for your complete staff to recreate your project while you are available for support. If the appropriate environment is not available for the whole group to participate, then you might want to choose a fishbowl procedure and have volunteers perform each step of the process while others observe. Your teachers and staff will now have observed the process twice.

Break (15 min.)

Have each member of the staff use one of their 3x5 cards to write down a question she/he may have at this time about the E-Tool. Use turning in the cards as the exit for a fifteen-minute break. During the break, read through the questions and prepare answers.

Checking for Understanding (15 min.)

Answer the questions that were written on the exit cards and demonstrate using the newly created project where needed.

Independent Practice (90 – 120 min.)

This is the opportunity for your staff to create a project that is useful and relevant to their individual classrooms. Give them time to create on their own using the new E-Tool. After about sixty minutes, have them return to the group to process a group sharing.

Lunch (60–90 min.)

Think Pair Share (45–60 min.)

First give the staff time to share their new creations with partners and then share with the whole group.

Reflection (15 min.)

Have staff reconvene to reflect about the implications of this E-Tool. Let them discuss the benefits and drawbacks they may have found during their exploratory experience.

Break (15 min.)

Small Group Exploration (45 min.)

Your staff may enjoy learning about a few managerial E-Tools at this time. Choose three or four management E-Tools from this book and share them. Have the staff discuss the potential benefits of implementing a time-saving tidbit in their individual classrooms.

Closure (15 min.)

Discuss the day's events and end on a positive note. Discuss your expectations about the use of these E-Tools in the classroom. (An administrative walk-through is a nice, nonintimidating way to confirm implementation.) Have your staff complete an anonymous 3x5 exit card at this time, using a variety of exit questions such as:

> *What new thing did I learn today?*
>
> *How am I first going to use this technology tool?*
>
> *What questions or concerns do I still need to have addressed?*

If anyone would like a direct answer to a question or concern, they can add their names.

Collect the exit cards and read all of them, taking careful notes. Answer those people who requested a direct answer the very next day. Respond to the other questions/concerns at your next staff meeting or in an e-mail. This will show your staff that you truly have an interest in their using the E-Tools in the classroom as soon as possible. It will also support the fact that you care about their success.

Continue to stay involved in staff growth through the next professional development day. Remember that you will be doing walk-throughs periodically. During your walk-through, be prepared to look for the E-Tools that have been the focus of the professional development day. This will sustain staff interest that began during the professional development day.

Half-day (4 Hour) Plan

Anticipatory Set (15 – 20 min.)

Preview the new instructional E-Tool using an example from this publication. Have teachers brainstorm ways to use this technology in their classrooms. If the presenter has an opportunity to create his or her own example of the E-Tool being demonstrated, specific to the district, building, or discipline of the group, the preview will have more impact. For example, create a cartoon using GoAnimate and give the characters the names of certain staff. This gives the staff a more thorough and entertaining example of the E-Tool.

Procedures (60 min.)

Using the tutorials provided, model each step of the process in creating a new project. This is the heart of your lesson, so you want to be sure that it's creative and motivational. Pause for questions and give a thorough explanation of each step of the process.

Guided Practice 30 min:

The guided practice portion of your lesson may take on a different look depending on your situation. If you are teaching in a lab setting or have access to a wireless environment, this is a great opportunity for your complete staff to recreate your project while you are available for support. If the appropriate environment is not available for the whole group to participate, then you might want to choose a fishbowl procedure and have volunteers perform each step of the process while others observe. Your teachers and staff will now have observed the process twice.

Break (15 min.)

Have each member of the staff use one of their 3x5 cards to write down a question she/he may have at this time about the E-Tool. Use turning in the cards as the exit for a fifteen-minute break. During the break, read through the questions and prepare answers.

Independent Practice (60 min.)

Take the first few minutes to answer the questions that were on the exit cards from the break. Then give the staff time to create a project on their own using the instructional E-Tool. After sixty minutes, have them return to the group to share what they have accomplished.

Reflection (30 min.)

Give the staff time to share their new creations and discuss with their colleagues.

Small Group Exploration (30 min.)

Your teachers and staff may enjoy learning about a few managerial E-Tools at this time. Choose three or four management E-Tools from this book and share them. Have the staff discuss the potential benefits of implementing a time-saving tidbit in their individual classrooms.

Closure (15 min.)

Discuss the day's events and end on a positive note. Discuss your expectations about the use of these E-Tools in the classroom. (An administrative walk-through is a nice, nonintimidating way to confirm implementation.) Have your staff fill out an anonymous 3x5 exit card at this time. If anyone would like a direct answer to a question or concern, they can add their names.

Another closure activity might be to include the following three questions on an exit card:

What new thing did I learn today?

How am I first going to use this technology tool?

What questions or concerns do I still need to have addressed?

Collect the exit cards and read all of them, taking careful notes. Answer those people who requested a direct answer the very next day. Respond to the other questions or concerns at your next staff meeting or in an e-mail. This will show your staff that you truly have an interest in them using the E-Tools in the classroom as soon as possible. It will also support the fact that you care about their success. Continue to stay involved in staff growth through the next professional development day. Remember that you will be doing walk-throughs periodically. During your walk-through, be prepared to look for the E-Tools that have been the focus of the professional development day. This will sustain staff interest that began during the professional development day.

Full-day (8 Hour) E-ProDev Plan

This agenda should be handed out prior to any E-ProDev day (or potential snow day). Again, the agenda is broken into specific time segments so that you can pick and choose sections that fit your professional development day schedule. You will want to tell the teachers ahead of time where you want them to post their work. Some suggestions include submitting via e-mail, uploading to the E-ProDev website (http://www.furmanr.com), posting on the school district website, or using a free forum.

Anticipatory Set (30 min.)

Answer the following brainstorming questions:

1. What types of instructional technology do you currently use in your classroom?

2. What are your classroom goals or class mission statement?

3. What technology do you think could help you to achieve your mission?

4. In which ways do you think technology would not be helpful in achieving your mission?

5. In what ways do you think technology can be used as a tool for students to learn, rather than just as a presentation tool?

Procedures Part 1 (30 min.)

Find the title of the E-Tool that was chosen by your professional development administrator or team. Review the first example of the E-Tool listed on http://www.furmanr.com. Read through the tutorial in this book that corresponds to the E-Tool example. Answer the following questions:

1. How do you see this instructional E-Tool being used in your classroom?

2. What do you see as the roadblocks to using this technology?

3. How can we remove these barriers so that you can use this technology?

4. What do you think you need to learn to be able to use this technology?

Guided Practice (30 min.)

Preplan a lesson in which you will use the E-Tool. Consider the following questions:

1. What are the goals for the lesson?

2. What is the essential question you want the class to be able to answer by the end of the lesson?

3. What additional technology would be useful for this type of lesson or objective? Why?

4. What are the benefits of using this E-Tool as compared to traditional teaching methods?

5. What will the students be creating using this technology?

6. Write a detailed plan outlining what you/your students wish to create using this technology. (If the outcome is a student project, the teacher will create an example.)

Independent Practice (100 min.)

Review the tutorial in this book that corresponds to the E-Tool chosen by your professional development administrator. Using the prescribed E-Tool, create the project that you will use in your lesson. If this is an example to be used with your students, make sure it is complete and follows all of the rules that you expect your students to follow. If this is a tutorial for your students, then make sure it is simple enough for your students to completely understand as they work through it independently. Upload the finished product (or a URL to the finished product) to the location designated by your administrator.

Procedures Part 2 (30 min.)

Review the example of the second E-Tool listed on http://www.furmanr.com. Read through the tutorial in this book that corresponds to this example. Answer the following questions:

1. How do you see this instructional E-Tool being used in your classroom?

2. What do you see as the roadblocks to using this technology?

3. How can we remove these barriers so that you can use this technology?

4. What do you think you need to learn to be able to use this technology?

Guided Practice (30 min.)

Preplan a second lesson in which you will use the E-Tool. Consider the following questions:

1. What are the goals for the lesson?

2. What is the essential question you want the class to be able to answer by the end of the lesson?

3. What type of technology would be useful for this type of lesson or objective? Why?

4. What are the benefits of using this E-Tool as compared to traditional teaching methods?

5. What will the students be creating using this technology?

6. Write a detailed plan outlining what you/your students wish to create using this technology. (If the outcome is a student project, the teacher will create an example.)

Independent Practice (100 min.)

Review the tutorial found in this book that corresponds to the second E-Tool chosen by your professional development administrator. Using the second E-Tool, create the project that you will use in your lesson. If this is an example to be used with your students, make sure it is complete and follows all of the rules that you expect your students to follow. If this is a tutorial for your students, then make sure it is simple enough for your students to completely understand as they work through it independently. Upload the finished product (or a URL to the finished product) to the location designated by your administrator.

Exploration (40 min.)

Choose two or three management E-Tools from this book and review them. Answer the following questions:

1. What do you see as the benefit of this E-Tool?

2. How would this E-Tool help you with your job?

3. What are some creative ways you could see this E-Tool being used:

   a. In the classroom?

   b. In the community?

   c. With parents?

   d. With fellow teachers?

   e. Other?

Year-long Plan with Technology as the Focus

This year-long plan assumes that the average district plans for approximately ten professional development days. The assumption is also that two of those days would be in the beginning of the year and two would be at the end of the year. Of course, every district has its own calendar; therefore this year-long plan is merely a suggestion and can easily be modified to fit your schedule. Two E-ProDev days have been included, but use of the E-ProDev alternative is also optional. An E-Tool, or in some cases several E-Tools, have been selected for each in-service day. These can be interchanged to suit the needs of your staff.

There are no prerequisites for learning each E-Tool. However, all of the E-Tools have a corresponding tutorial in the following chapters.

Day 1

Time: Beginning of the Year
Agenda: Half-day Agenda
Tool(s): GoAnimate

To create a motivational anticipatory set, consider giving the audience a "sneak peek" at some of the clever tools they will be using. Create several examples of the various E-Tools you plan to use throughout the year. (You may also use the examples on the http://www.furmanr.com website.) Use these examples to grab the attention of the staff and get them excited about the possibilities of using these new instructional technology tools.

During this first day, announce the year-long theme of instructional technology tools. You may get moans and groans or cheers, but regardless, this is the time to dispel the myths. Use the information in the Instructional Technology Tools chapter to prepare this "myth-busting" discussion. The day should be fun and exciting, but should also set your expectations for the use of technology in the classroom. At this time, touch on the fact that you will expect to see instructional technology tools being used when you do your walk-throughs of the building.

Day 2

Time: Beginning of Year
Agenda: Full-day Agenda
Tool(s): Glogster

Make this day a full working day. Give the staff the opportunity to dive deeply into the Glogster tool. This day will solidify the tone for the importance of instructional technology in your school.

Day 3

Time: Fall Session
Agenda: Two Half-day Agendas
Tool(s): WizIQ and WebQuest

This should be another work session. The benefit of using two half-day agendas is that your staff will learn two instructional tools instead of one. This will give them a good feeling about getting a lot of information in a short amount of time.

Be careful in selecting the tools. You don't want to overwhelm your staff, especially if it includes many *digital immigrants*—the term often used to label those persons born before the digital era, who may need more help with technology. Maybe choosing one challenging E-Tool and one less difficult E-Tool will ease your staff into the world of technology.

Day 4

Time: E-ProDev Day 1
Agenda: E-ProDev Day Agenda
Tool(s): Masher and Bubbl.us

Day 5

Time: Halfway and Celebration
Agenda: Half-day Agenda
Tool(s): Zunal

This day needs to be a celebration of the halfway point in the professional development schedule. The first half of the day should be a typical half-day professional development agenda. The second half of the day should be a sharing of all the projects that the teachers have created to date. Let them share with each other their hardships in creating their projects and how they fared when using those projects in the classroom. Let them discuss among themselves the positives and negatives they found while trying to use the tools.

Day 6

Time: E-ProDev Day 2
Agenda: E-ProDev Day Agenda
Tool(s): Hot Potatoes and ChartGizmo

Day 7

Time: Spring Session
Agenda: Full-day Agenda
Tool(s): Museum Box

This session needs to have a motivational "feel." In a typical professional development calendar, this could be the first session in the spring, so it is important to set the climate for the remainder of the year. During this session, it would also be good to gather feedback on the second E-ProDev day. Get the staff to share some of their creations as well as give you ideas for enhancing future E-ProDev days.

Day 8

Time: Spring Session
Agenda: Two Half-day Agendas
Tool(s): TargetMap/quikmaps and VUVOX

This is another hardworking session. At this time it might be a good idea to set the stage for the final two sessions. Give your staff the directives for the last two professional development days, and let them start to think about and/or develop their presentation.

Day 9

Time: End of Year
Agenda: Full-day Agenda—Special End of Year Agenda
Tool(s): All Previous Tools

Give the teachers the directive to prepare or enhance one of their projects for a presentation to the staff. Give them the day to work on creating a new project using any of the tools that they learned during the whole year. The second half of the day should be the beginning of the presentations.

Day 10

Time: End of Year
Agenda: Full-day Agenda—Special End of Year Agenda
Tool(s): All Previous Tools

Finish the presentations and have a final talk about the great strides the staff has made using technology in their classrooms. Be positive and get them looking forward to the next year's theme. Show off your staff's hard work by adding links to their projects on the district website, or create a staff-only website where you can share projects. They deserve the credit.

Tutorials

The tutorials in this section are meant to be used by teachers and students to quickly learn how to use a specific E-Tool. These tutorials are simple, yet detailed enough to give a solid understanding of the capabilities of the program or website. By following the steps in the tutorial, the user should end with one complete project and a solid foundation of how to use the program.

The tutorial that you will be using for each in-service day should be printed and distributed to the staff. It will be their guide to using the program when they are working independently on their projects. Also, be sure to mention that the same tutorials can be used in the classrooms with students. E-Tool tutorials that are to be used during E-ProDev days need to be reproduced in advance and added to the packet that the teachers will use at home or a remote location.

Each tutorial can be used with any subject matter or instructional discipline. Project rubrics can be found in the Appendix. These tutorials are not exhaustive, and it is suggested that you "tweak" them to suit the needs of your students.

WebQuest

Description
WebQuest allows you to create lessons solely (or mostly) based on information found on the Internet.

Resources
http://webquest.org/index.php

How does it work?
Step 1: To begin, click Create WebQuests from the menu on the left side of the page.

Step 2: The next page provides information about different varieties of WebQuests (some of which cost money). To create an original and free WebQuest, scroll to the bottom of the page and click WebQuest Design Process. There are also templates you can download for ideas about how to organize your WebQuest.

Step 3: A new page will appear that describes the process of creating a WebQuest step-by-step, including links to brief documents illustrating each step, so that you can create a WebQuest that is appropriate for your lesson goals.

Step 4: Follow the steps to create a WebQuest from a lesson plan that you have already developed.

For Example:

- Find a URL that the students can investigate to gain information about a specific topic. Use that URL as the basis of your new WebQuest.

- The second part of your WebQuest could lead to several other useful sites that you wish your class to explore. Preplan questions for the students to turn in to you at the conclusion of the WebQuest.

Zunal

Description
Zunal is Web-based software for creating fast and efficient WebQuests.

Resources
http://www.zunal.com

How to begin?
Step 1: Go to www.zunal.com

Step 2: Log on using your team's information.

Step 3: Click on Create a New WebQuest.

Step 4: Click on Create a New WebQuest from Scratch.

Step 5: Title your WebQuest with your topic's name.

Step 6: Click Save Now.

Step 7: Click Continue.

Step 8: Review instructions below and on the Zunal Creation Page.

How do I add resources?
Step 1: Find or make your resource. Examples: PowerPoint presentation, artwork, graphic organizer, etc.

Step 2: Click on Add/Attach a File.

Step 3: Browse for your file.

Step 4: Click on your file.

Step 5: Write a short description of the file's purpose in the window provided.

Step 6: Click on Save Now.

Step 7: Click on Continue.

How do I insert a website?
Step 1: In the bar at the top of your Web browser, highlight the website URL and then right-click on it.

Step 2: Go to your WebQuest page and click on button labeled Update.

Step 3: Paste the URL into the page by right-clicking and selecting Paste from the menu.

Step 4: Click on Save Now.

Step 5: Click on Continue.

How do I upload an image?

Step 1: Go to a search engine site.

Step 2: Type in a key word(s) that describes your topic.

Step 3: Click on Images in the upper tool bar.

Step 4: Click on the image you would like to use.

Step 5: Right-click on the image.

Step 6: Select Save Picture As from the menu.

Step 7: Save the image to your hard drive using the scrollbar at the top of the page and choosing the location to which you wish to save this picture.

Step 8: Go back to your WebQuest page and click on Upload Image.

Step 9: Browse to find your picture in the location where you originally chose to save it.

Step 10: Click Save Now.

Step 11: Click Continue.

Step 12: Copy and paste the URL of the web page where you found each picture into the section where you wish to use it. Do this by highlighting the website URL and then right-clicking on it. Click on Update and then paste the URL into the page. Click on Save Now. Click Continue.

Glogster

Description

Glogster allows you to create a blog (referred to as a Glog on this website) using various text and media to create a one-page poster.

Resources

http://www.glogster.com/

How to begin?

Step 1: To create an account, Fill in the corresponding information for each box and then click Create Account.

Step 2: The page that appears is your profile or "dashboard."

Step 3: Similar to other social networking sites, you can add friends, communicate via messages, and update your "status" or how you are feeling/what you are doing.

What can I do with my dashboard page?

Step 1: To set your status, click in the speech bubble at the top of the page next to your nickname. Type in what you would like to share with others and click enter/return.

Step 2: Your messages can be found on the left side of the page under Messages. You can send and receive messages with other Glogster users.

Step 3: To chat with other Glogster users who are online right now, click the doodletoo chat icon next to Messages. This allows you to type or write (using your mouse) messages to anyone else who is currently using the site.

Step 4: New changes that have been made to the website can be found on the right side of the page under Glog Alerts.

Step 5: Your friends can be found on the bottom right side of the page.

Step 6: To add friends, click on Show All inside the Friends box.

Step 7: This page will show you all of your current friends. To add friends, click on Find New Friends at the top left of the page next to [Your Nickname]'s Friends. You can search friends by demographics or by nickname.

Step 8: To return to your dashboard page at any time, click the My Dashboard icon in the panel of icons at the top of the page.

How can I create a Glog?

Step 1: On your dashboard page, click Create New Glog. A sample Glog page will appear.

Step 2: To change the background of the Glog, click on Wall in the panel of icons on the left side of the page.

Step 3: A Glog Wall dialog box will appear. You can browse different colors, patterns, and pictures to use as your background. Click on the one that you would like and it will appear in the right pane of the dialog box.

Step 4: Click Use It and the selected image will become the background to your Glog. Click on the red X in the top right corner of the box to return to your Glog.

How can I add text, images, etc. to my Glog?

Step 1: To add text, click on Text from the panel of icons on the left side of the page.

Step 2: A text dialog box will appear, where you can browse different ways to display your text. Click on the one that you would like and it will appear in the right pane of the dialog box.

Step 3: Click Use It and it will appear on your Glog. Click on the red X in the top right corner of the box to return to your Glog.

Step 4: Repeat Steps 1–3 to add graphics to your Glog. Start by clicking on Graphics from the same panel of icons on the left side of the page.

Step 5: You can also add images, videos, and sounds to your Glog using files of your own or by searching online.

Step 6: Start by clicking the corresponding icon (Image, Video, or Sound) from the panel on the left side of the page.

Step 7: A dialog box will appear. You can choose how to upload the image, video, or sound. You can upload your own (one that is saved on your computer), add a link to another online source, or "grab" an image, video, or sound using a webcam. Click on the appropriate option.

Step 8: Follow the instructions (click on image, insert address, etc.) to add your media and it will appear in the panel on the right side of the dialog box.

Step 9: Click Use It and it will appear on your Glog. Click on the red X in the top right corner of the box to return to your Glog.

How can I change or edit the text, images, etc. on my Glog?

Step 1: To edit text, click on the image that is holding the text box.

Step 2: Click Edit in the panel above the box. This allows you to type in the text box.

Step 3: To change the color of the image around the text box, click the multicolored icon (second from the left) in the panel above the box.

Step 4: A Change Color dialog box will appear. You can click on different colors to change the background image. After choosing the color you want, click Apply.

Step 5: You can add a hyperlink, change the color and font of the text, and add effects to the image using the remaining three icons and following the same steps.

Step 6: When you have finished making the changes you want to your text, click OK in the panel above the image.

Step 7: To edit a graphic, click on the graphic.

Step 8: A panel similar to the one for text will appear. You can change the color, add a hyperlink, or add effects to the graphic. When you have finished editing the graphic, click OK.

Step 9: You can bring in the image to the front or put the image behind another graphic (or other media) by clicking on the second (Bring It Forward) or third (Put It Behind) icon from the left in the panel above the graphic.

Step 10: To copy the graphic, click the Clone icon (two boxes, one in front of the other) in the panel above the graphic.

Step 11: You can also cancel your changes or delete the graphic by using the last two icons in the panel.

Step 12: You can move any of your text, images, or other media around on your Glog by clicking on the media and dragging it to where you want it.

How can I share my Glog with others?

Step 1: To see what your Glog will look like to others, click Preview at the top of the page.

Step 2: When finished, click Back to Edit. (You can still make changes to your Glog at any time.)

Step 3: When finished with your Glog, click Save or Publish at the top of the page.

Step 4: You can give your Glog a title, a category, and any tags you would like so that people can search your Glog. There will also be a Web address (URL) that will belong only to this Glog, so you can share your Glog that way.

Step 5: Choose whether you would like your Glog to be public (anyone can see it) or private (only you and the friends you have identified on the site can see it) by clicking the corresponding icon in the right panel of the box.

Step 6: Click Save to publish your Glog.

Step 7: A dialog box will appear for you to choose other ways to share your Glog, such as through social networking sites (e.g. Facebook, Twitter), embedding code into a website, or simply copying and pasting the URL of your Glog into an e-mail.

Step 8: At the bottom of the box, you can choose to view the Glog, edit the Glog, or return to your dashboard page.

WizIQ

Description
WizIQ provides tools for online teaching and virtual classrooms.

Resources
http://www.wiziq.com/

How to begin?
Step 1: To begin, enter the corresponding information into the boxes on the right side of the page to create your free account.

Step 2: Click Sign Up.

Step 3: You will receive an e-mail from WizIQ with a link in it. You must click on that link to verify your e-mail address and finish creating your account.

Step 4: After clicking on the e-mail link, a confirmation page will appear to verify your account. Click Return to the Dashboard.

Step 5: A new page will appear. You will be asked what you will be using WizIQ for. Click on the appropriate choice, and then click Submit.

How can I create an online class?
Step 1: Click Schedule a Class at the top of the page.

Step 2: A new page will appear. You can enter the title, date, time, description, and privacy settings for the class. When finished, click Schedule and Continue.

Step 3: The next page that appears will be your class page. You can share your class using the icons at the top of the page. Options include Twitter, Facebook, and Stumble Upon, or you can add the class to your Google or Outlook calendar.

Step 4: To invite people to your class, click on Invite Attendees from the menu on the left side of the page. You can choose attendees from your contacts or enter e-mail addresses. Compose a message if you choose to and click Invite Contacts.

Step 5: To edit information about the class, click Class Information from the menu on the left side of the page. You can edit the title and description of the class. Click Save.

Step 6: To edit settings for the class (e.g., maximum number of attendees, duration, audio/video access, etc.), click Recoding and Class Settings from the menu on the left side of the page. Change settings as needed and click Save.

Step 7: Comments can be posted about the class under the Comments tab on the menu on the left side of the page.

Step 8: Attendees can provide feedback about the class after it is over. The feedback can be found under the Feedback tab on the menu on the left side of the page.

Step 9: To change the day or time of the class, click Change Class Time in the menu on the left side of the page. Make any necessary changes and click Update. This will automatically update the attendees about the change. You can also include a message to the attendees about the changes.

Step 10: To cancel the class, click Cancel Class in the menu on the left side of the page. You can include a message if you would like to prior to canceling the class.

Step 11: When the class is ready, click Launch Class at the top right corner of the page.

Museum Box

Description

Museum Box allows you to describe an event, person or historical period by placing items in a virtual box. You can display anything from a text file to a movie.

Subject Area:

Designed for second through twelfth-grade students. Can be used for any subject with an emphasis on gathering information around a topic.

Resources

http://museumbox.e2bn.org/creator/

How to begin?

Step 1: Give your Museum Box a title and description.

Step 2: Click on an individual box. A new page for a "cube" will appear. Give that cube a title.

Step 3: Add text, images, sounds, videos, files and/or links to each side of the cube.

Step 4: Add a caption below your completed cube.

Step 5: When you are finished with the cube, click Close and repeat these steps to add another cube.

How do I add text, images, etc?

Step 1: Click on the icon at the bottom of the page describing what you want to add.

Step 2: Select the item you wish to add, whether by typing in the text, searching the site's gallery, uploading your own image, etc.

Step 3: After you have loaded what you want to use, click Add to Drawer.

Step 4: Click Close.

Step 5: Go to the box that you wanted to decorate and click My Drawer.

Step 6. Click Add to Cube.

Step 7. Click on the X to close your drawer.

****Each of your boxes must have at least one side filled with text and another side filled with another item (image, sound, video, file, or link). You may fill all six sides if you have sufficient time and content to do so. ****

How can I use images, videos, or sound that I find on the Web in my Museum Box?

Step 1. Find the image, sound, or video files online.

Step 2. Save the media to your hard drive. For images, right-click on the image and select Save As from the menu. For sound and video files, you will have to find a Download option on the website and save the file to your hard drive as an mp3, .flv, .mpg, .avi, .wmv, or .mp4 file type.

Step 3. Click Save In and save in a location that you will remember.

Step 4. Go back to your Museum Box. Click on the icon representing whatever type of media you are uploading.

Step 5. Click Upload.

Step 6. Click Browse.

Step 7. Click Look In.

Step 8. Find the location where you are saving files for this project.

Step 9. Find your media file and click on it.

Step 10. Click Open.

Step 11. Click Upload.

Step 12. Click on the file you wish to use so that it shows up in the highlighted green box and follow the instruction above for Adding Images.

How do I attach files I already have?

Step 1. Click File.

Step 2. Click Upload.

Step 3. Click Browse.

Step 4. Find your file and click on it.

Step 5. Click Open.

Step 6. Click Upload.

How do I add a link?

Step 1. Click Links.

Step 2. Type or paste your link (URL) into the box labeled Address.

Step 3. Give your link a title.

Step 4. Click Save.

How do I save my Museum Box?

Step 1. Click on Save.

Step 2. If not completed in earlier steps, give the box a title and description and click Save.

Step 3. Click on Submit.

Step 4. Click on Submit My Box.

You must do this for each box. You should only save if you are not done with the box. Do not submit anything unless it is 100% complete. You will not be able to make changes once you submit.

How do I get back to my box on another day or to see if it has been approved?

Step 1: Go to http://museumbox.e2bn.org/creator/

Step 2. Click on Load from the icons at the top of the page.

Step 3. Click on the title of *your* box.

Step 4. Click Load and your box will appear.

GoAnimate

Description

GoAnimate allows you to create animated videos.

Resources

http://goanimate.com/

How to begin?

Step 1: To create an account, click Sign Up at the top of the page and choose Basic.

Step 2: Fill in the corresponding information for each box, and click Create My Account when finished.

Step 3: To begin, click on your username at the top of the page. A drop-down menu will appear. Click Your Home.

Step 4: Click on Make Your 1st Cartoon! in the middle of the page.

Step 5: The first time that you use the website, a tutorial will walk you through the process of creating a video, including adding the background, characters, and voices. This will help you get started.

How can I add effects to my video?

Step 1: To add speech bubbles, click on the Speech Bubble icon (second from the left) in the panel of icons at the top left of the page.

Step 2: Click on the type of speech bubble that you would like, and it will appear in your scene.

Step 3: You can type what will appear in the speech bubble into the box on the left side of the page.

Step 4: To add objects to your scene, click on the Objects icon (looks like a basketball; third from the right) in the panel of icons at the top left of the page.

Step 5: Click on the object that you want to add to your scene. It will appear in your scene, and you can click and drag it where you want it.

Step 6: If you add the object to a character (e.g., the character is now holding it), a box will appear that will ask you to add the object to the character in every scene. Click Yes or No.

Step 7: To add sound, click on the Sounds icon (looks like a music note; second from the right) in the panel of icons at the top left of the page.

Step 8: You can browse music and sound effects, or upload your own sound. Click the sound that you want and it will appear in the scene map at the bottom of the page.

Step 9: You can edit the length of time that the sound plays by placing your cursor at the end of the box within your scene map. A double arrow will appear that you can drag across your other scenes.

Step 10: To add other effects, click the Effects icon (FX; farthest right) in the panel of icons at the top left of the page.

Step 11: Browse a variety of effects (e.g. earthquakes, curtain call, etc.) to add to each scene. Click on the effect(s) that you would like.

Step 12: Each effect that you add to a scene will appear in the top right corner of the page with an FX icon. To edit or delete the effect, click on the FX icon and choose the appropriate action.

How can I edit my video?

Step 1: To copy, paste, or undo any changes that you have made to your video, use the corresponding icons at the top of the page.

Step 2: To change the size of the video within the page, use the bar to the bottom left of the video. Click and drag the icon along the bar to change the video's size.

Step 3: To preview your video, click Preview at the top right corner of the page.

How can I share my video?

Step 1: To save your video, click Save at the top right corner of the page.

Step 2: A Save Your Animation dialog box will appear. You can enter a title for your video, tags so that your video can be searched for online, and a description of your video.

Step 3: You can choose whether your video is a draft or final version, as well as whether you would like it to be public or private, by clicking the corresponding icons on the right side of the box.

Step 4: Click Save to return to your video, or click Save and Share to share your video with others.

Step 5: If you click Save and Share, a page will appear that allows you to choose how to share your video.

Step 6: Options on the right side of the page include uploading your video to a social networking site (e.g., Facebook, Twitter, etc.), sharing an address link for others to view the video, embedding code into a website to share the video, or uploading the video to YouTube.

Step 7: The box in the center of the page allows you to sign in to your e-mail account and import the e-mail addresses of the people with whom you'd like to share your video.

Prezi

Description

Prezi allows you to create presentations using a single online space so that you and others viewing your presentation can see how ideas connect.

Resources

http://prezi.com/

How to begin?

Step 1: To create your own free account, click on Sign Up at the top right corner of the page.

Step 2: The page will show you three options for your account. The first column is the free option. To use this one, click Get at the bottom of the column.

Step 3: On the registration page, enter the corresponding information into the boxes. Click the box to agree to the terms of service, and then click Register and Continue.

Step 4: A dialog box will appear. Here you choose how to start using Prezi. You can watch a tutorial video, go through three lessons, look at already created Prezis, or start using Prezi. Click the option that you would like to start with.

Step 5: You can always go back to the lessons to learn how to use different features of Prezi by clicking on the Learn tab at the top of the page.

How can I create a Prezi?

Step 1: Click the Your Prezis tab at the top of the page.

Step 2: To create a new Prezi, click New Prezi at the top left corner of the page.

Step 3: A dialog box will appear. Enter a title and description for your Prezi. When finished, click New Prezi.

Step 4: A dialog box will appear. You can choose to go through a brief tutorial on how to create a Prezi by clicking Start. To get out of the tutorial, click the X at the top right corner.

Step 5: To begin creating, click anywhere on the page that you'd like to add an idea.

Step 6: A blue circle will appear. To type an idea, click on Edit at the bottom left of the blue circle.

Step 7: A box will appear into which you can type. You can choose the style of title or body text that you would like from the options to the right of the box. When finished, click OK.

Step 8: To edit your title, click on it. The blue circle will appear again.

Step 9: You can change the size of the title by clicking on the + to make it larger or the – to make it smaller. You can also change the title's orientation by clicking the outer circle of the blue circle. This will let you rotate the title. To move the title in the space in the page, click on the hand symbol in the center of the circle and drag the title to where you want it. You may need to click the icon a second time to exit that icon.

Step 10: To change the details of the body (main) text of an idea, click on the text and then follow the same process described in Step 9.

Step 11: To add another idea, click somewhere in the page and follow Steps 6-9 above.

Step 12: Continue to add ideas until you have included all of the information that you would like to have in your Prezi.

How can I edit my Prezi with colors, images, etc.?

Step 1: At the top left corner of the page, there is a circle surrounded by smaller circles with different options. These circles allow you to edit your Prezi in many ways.

Step 2: To change colors and fonts, click on Colors.

Step 3: Several options will appear that will change the colors and fonts of your Prezi.

Step 4: To customize your Prezi, click on Theme Wizard. A dialog box will appear for you to choose specific colors and other options. Follow the directions, clicking Next at the bottom of the page to progress through the wizard. When finished, click Done.

Step 5: To return to the main navigation circle, click on the arrow above Colors.

Step 6: To add images and other media, click Insert.

Step 7: Several options will appear for inserting a file, YouTube video, or image. Click the appropriate option and follow the directions to insert the media. You may have to copy and paste a link or browse your computer for a file or image.

Step 8: You can also add shapes, such as lines and arrows, by clicking Shapes. Click on the shape that you would like to add to your Prezi and then click in the Prezi to insert the shape.

Step 9: To return to the main navigation circle, click on the arrow above Insert.

Step 10: To frame your text, click Frame.

Step 11: Several options will appear for framing your text with a box, circle, or brackets. Click on the appropriate choice, and then click and drag to the Prezi to insert the frame. You can adjust the frame's size and orientation by clicking and dragging the edge of the frame.

Step 12: To return to the main navigation circle, click on the arrow above Frame.

How can I organize my Prezi?

Step 1: Click on Path from the navigation circles at the top left of the page.

Step 2: Options will appear to help you establish the order in which your ideas are presented.

Step 3: Click on Capture View and the number 1 will appear within a circle. You can click and drag the 1 to the first idea you would like to present.

Step 4: To add the next idea, click Capture View again and a 2 will appear within a circle. Click and drag the 2 to the second idea that you would like to present.

Step 5: Repeat the Capture View step to create a path for all of the ideas on the Prezi.

Step 6: To delete or start over with your path, click Delete All.

How can I share my Prezi?

Step 1: You can invite people to edit your Prezi by clicking Meeting at the top of the page and then clicking Invite to Edit.

Step 2: A dialog box will appear with a link that you can share with others. They are then able to edit your Prezi.

Step 3: To use your Prezi for an online presentation, click Meeting at the top of the page and then click Start Online Presentation.

Step 4: A dialog box will appear with a link that you can share with others to view your presentation.

Step 5: You can share your Prezi in other ways when you finish it.

What do I do when I am finished with my Prezi?

Step 1: When finished, click Exit at the top of the page.

Step 2: You will return to the website where your Prezi is stored.

Step 3: Using the icons on the right side of the page, you can edit, save, download, or delete your Prezi.

Step 4: You can also use the arrow button below your Prezi to go through the presentation.

Step 5: To share your Prezi using Twitter, Facebook, etc., click the appropriate icon to the bottom left of your Prezi.

Step 6: Below your Prezi, you can also choose privacy settings. If you choose public, people will be able to make comments on your Prezi. A private Prezi cannot be viewed by anyone but you and those to whom you give permission to view by sharing a link.

Webspiration

Description

Webspiration allows you to create lessons and activities using diagrams, outlines, and other documents.

Resources

http://www.inspiration.com/

How to begin?

Step 1: To begin, click on Free Trials at the top right corner of the page.

Step 2: Scroll down the page until you find Webspiration Classroom. Click on the appropriate free trial for you: administrator (with ten student accounts) or a single educator account.

Step 3: A new page will appear where you can enter the corresponding information for your free trial. Click Create Account.

Step 4: A menu will appear from which you can choose the type of activity to create: Diagram, Outline, Document Templates, or Open an Existing Activity.

How can I create a diagram?

Step 1: From the main screen, click Diagram.

Step 2: A blank canvas will appear with a bubble in the center. You can click inside the bubble and type in the main idea for the diagram.

Step 3: To move the bubble, click and drag it around the canvas.

Step 4: To resize the bubble, click and drag the square icons around the bubble to the desired size.

Step 5: To add another bubble, click Create from the toolbar at the top of the page.

Step 6: A new bubble will appear that will be connected to the main bubble. You can enter text, move it, and resize it in the same manner as you did the first bubble.

Step 7: Repeat Steps 5 and 6 to continue adding bubbles to your diagram.

Step 8: To link one bubble to another, preexisting bubble, click on the first bubble, then click Link from the toolbar at the top of the page. An arrow will appear. Drag the arrow the bubble you want to link and click on it.

Step 9: To create a bubble that is not connected to other bubbles, click the RapidFire icon from the toolbar at the top of the page.

Step 10: To change the shape of the bubbles, browse from the menu on the left side of the page and click on different bubbles to find one that works for your diagram. You can browse the available shapes by either clicking on the drop-down menu above them or using the arrow icons below them.

Step 11: To edit the text or bubbles to change the color or line thickness, click on Effects from the toolbar at the top of the page. Click on the appropriate menu to edit and then choose the edits you would like to make. (A formatting toolbar is also available on the bottom of the page.)

Step 12: To insert a hyperlink (URL) into your diagram, click Hyperlink from the toolbar at the top of the page. A dialog box will appear. Enter a hyperlink. Click OK.

Step 13: To share your diagram, click Invite from the toolbar at the top of the page. A dialog box will appear. Enter the contact information for people with whom you would like to share the diagram. Click OK.

Step 14: Others can comment on your diagram or chat with you using the tabs on the right side of the page.

Step 15: To view your diagram in outline format, click Outline View from the toolbar at the top of the page. To go back to diagram format, click Diagram View.

How can I create an outline?

Step 1: From the main menu, click Outline.

Step 2: A blank page will appear. Click where it says Main Idea and type in the main idea of your outline.

Step 3: To add a topic below the main idea, click Topic from the toolbar at the top of the page. A topic line will appear below the main idea. Click in it and type in the topic.

Step 4: To add a subtopic below a topic, click Subtopic from the toolbar at the top of the page. A subtopic line will appear below the topic. Click in it and type in the subtopic.

Step 5: To change the indent or level (e.g., topic vs. subtopic) of a line, click on the line and click on one of the arrow icons on the top of the page.

Step 6: To add a note that is within a topic or subtopic, click Note from the toolbar at the top of the page. A line will appear without an outline indicator (e.g., I, II, A, etc.). Type in notes for that topic or subtopic.

Step 7: To insert a hyperlink into your outline, click Hyperlink from the toolbar at the top of the page. A dialog box will appear. Enter a hyperlink. Click OK.

Step 8: To share your outline, click Invite from the toolbar at the top of the page. A dialog box will appear. Enter the contact information for people with whom you would like to share the diagram. Click OK.

Step 9: Others can comment on your outline or chat with you using the tabs on the right side of the page.

Step 10: To view your outline in diagram format, click Diagram View from the toolbar at the top of the page. To go back to outline format, click Outline View.

How can I use the document templates?

Step 1: From the main screen, click Starter Docs.

Step 2: A menu will appear that includes a variety of already created (or started) diagrams and outlines. Browse the menu and choose an appropriate document.

Step 3: Edit the diagram or outline using the same steps above to change the document to suit your needs.

Webspiriation has a 30 day free trial. If after 30 days you find this software useful it is suggested that you purchase the software. After 30 days, your trial is over and web-based creations will be lost.

Hot Potatoes

Description

Hot Potatoes allows you to create a variety of online exercises, such as crossword puzzles, multiple choice questions, etc.

Resources

http://hotpot.uvic.ca/

How to begin?

Step 1: To download Hot Potatoes, click on the appropriate link under Downloads on the Hot Potatoes website.

Step 2: Follow the onscreen instructions to download the Hot Potatoes applications to your computer.

Step 3: Install and then open Hot Potatoes.

Step 4: You have several options to create an exercise: JCloze (fill-in-the-gap), JQuiz (quiz), JCross (crossword puzzle), JMatch (matching), and JMix (jumbled sentence).

Step 5: Once you have a set of exercises, you can combine them by using the Masher tool in the Hot Potatoes program.

How can I create a fill-in-the-gap exercise?

Step 1: On the main screen, click JCloze.

Step 2: Type the title of the exercise into the box next to the word Title.

Step 3: In the large box below the title, type in the full sentence(s) or paragraph(s).

Step 4: Highlight the word that would fill the gap, and click Gap at the bottom of the page.

Step 5: A dialog box will appear. You can choose to provide a clue to the answer as well as alternative answers that would also be correct.

Step 6: When finished, click OK. The word that would fill the gap is now italicized and red in color.

Step 7: To delete a gap, highlight the word for the gap and click Delete Gap at the bottom of the page.

Step 8: To delete all of the gaps that you have entered, click Clear Gaps.

Step 9: To insert a gap every X amount of words, click Auto Gap and then enter the interval (number of words) that you would like to set. Click OK.

Step 10: To see all of the gapped words (and clues and alternatives), click Show Words.

Step 11: To save your exercise, click the Save icon (third from the left) in the toolbar at the top of the page.

Step 12: You can also create a new exercise or open an existing exercise by clicking the corresponding icons in the toolbar.

Step 13: You can upload your exercise to a Hot Potatoes website by clicking the Export icon (fifth from the left) on the toolbar.

Step 14: To close the exercise and go back to the main screen, click the Close icon (red, down-facing arrow).

How can I create a quiz?

Step 1: On the main screen, click JQuiz.

Step 2: Type the title of the quiz in the box next to the word Title.

Step 3: Type the first question into the box next to Q1.

Step 4: To choose the type of answer (e.g., multiple choice, short answer, or multiple), click the arrow in the box to the right of the question. Select the type that you would like.

Step 5: Type in the answer options in the column under Answers. For more answer choices, click the top arrow icon under the Q1.

Step 6: In the column under Feedback, you can type in a word or phrase that will be shown after the student has chosen an answer, such as "Correct!" or "Try again."

Step 7: In the column under Settings, choose which answer(s) is (are) correct.

Step 8: To create a new question, click the top arrow icon next to Q1. (It will change to Q2, Q3, and so on for each new question.)

Step 9: Repeat Steps 3–8 for each new question.

Step 10: To save your quiz, click the Save icon (third from the left) in the toolbar at the top of the page.

Step 11: You can also create a new quiz or open an existing quiz by clicking the corresponding icons in the toolbar at the top of the screen.

Step 12: You can upload your quiz to a Hot Potatoes website by clicking the Export icon (fifth from the left) on the toolbar.

Step 13: To close the quiz and go back to the main screen, click the Close icon (red, down-facing arrow).

How can I create a crossword puzzle?

Step 1: On the main screen, click JCross.

Step 2: Type in the title of the crossword puzzle in the box under the word Title.

Step 3: Using the Grid Show option, you can type in the answers in the way that you want them to appear in the puzzle.

Step 4: To shift the puzzle in any direction on the grid, use the arrow icons at the bottom left of the page.

Step 5: To add clues for the puzzle, click the Add Clues icon at the left of the page.

Step 6: An Add Clues dialog box will appear. Click on the answer under either Across or Down. Type in the clue in the box below the answer.

Step 7: When finished, click OK.

Step 8: You can also change the layout of the words by clicking the Create a Grid Automatically icon on the toolbar (third from the right). This will randomize the layout of the puzzle while keeping the same words and clues.

Step 9: To save your puzzle, click the Save icon (third from the left) in the toolbar at the top of the page.

Step 10: You can also create a new puzzle or open an existing puzzle by clicking the corresponding icons on the toolbar.

Step 11: You can upload your puzzle to a Hot Potatoes website by clicking the Export icon (fifth from the left) on the toolbar.

Step 12: To close the puzzle and go back to the main screen, click the Close icon (red, down-facing arrow).

How can I create a matching exercise?

Step 1: On the main screen, click JMatch.

Step 2: Type in the title of the exercise into the box next to the word Title.

Step 3: Type in the one set of items in the left column under Left (ordered) Items.

Step 4: Type in the matching set of items in the right column under Right (jumbled) Items.

Step 5: The items in the left column will appear in the same order while the items in the right column will be mixed up. To keep any of the items in the right column in the same place that they are now, click the box next to the column on the right side, under Fix.

Step 6: To add rows of items, click the top arrow icon under Title.

Step 7: To save your exercise, click the Save icon (third from the left) in the toolbar at the top of the page.

Step 8: You can also create a new exercise or open an existing exercise by clicking the corresponding icons on the toolbar.

Step 9: You can upload your exercise to a Hot Potatoes website by clicking the Export icon (fifth from the left) in the toolbar.

Step 10: To close the exercise and go back to the main screen, click the Close icon (red, down-facing arrow).

How can I create a jumbled sentence exercise?

Step 1: On the main screen, click JMix.

Step 2: Type in the title (or directions) of the exercise into the box next to the word Title.

Step 3: Type in the target sentence into the box under Main Sentence.

Step 4: Type in any acceptable alternatives to the target sentence into the boxes under Alternate Sentences. To add more alternative sentences, click the top arrow icon.

Step 5: To save your exercise, click the Save icon (third from the left) in the toolbar at the top of the page.

Step 6: You can also create a new exercise or open an existing exercise by clicking the corresponding icons on the toolbar.

Step 7: You can upload your exercise to a Hot Potatoes website by clicking the Export icon (fifth from the left) on the toolbar.

Step 8: To close the exercise and go back to the main screen, click the Close icon (red, down-facing arrow).

How can I combine exercises?

Step 1: On the main screen, click The Masher.

Step 2: To insert exercises, click Add Files.

Step 3: A dialog box will appear. Browse your computer to find the appropriate files. Click the file of the exercise that you would like to insert and click Open.

Step 4: A second dialog box will appear that allows you to change the name of your exercise if you choose. Click OK.

Step 5: Repeat Steps 2–4 to insert additional exercises. The exercises will appear in the box.

Step 6: To change what your exercises will look like, click the Appearance tab at the top of the page. You can choose colors and make other changes (e.g., add graphics) to the appearance of your exercises.

Step 7: When ready to publish your exercises, click Build Unit at the bottom of the page.

Step 8: Once the unit is built, a dialog box will appear asking you if you would like to see your unit now. If you would like to see your exercises online, click Yes. If you would like to return to the main screen, click No.

VUVOX

Description
VUVOX allows you to create presentations using a variety of media.

Resources
http://www.vuvox.com/

How to begin?
Step 1: To begin, click Get a Free Account at the bottom left corner of the page.

Step 2: Enter all of the corresponding information for your account.

Step 3: Click Join Now.

Step 4: The next page that appears will be your page. You can choose to go through a tour of VUVOX using a channel that has been created as a sample. Otherwise, click Edit your Channel.

Step 5: To begin creating, click Create Something Now.

Step 6: You will see three options to choose from: Express (a fast, easy way to develop a presentation), Collage (allows you to create collages from various photos, videos, and interactive media), or Studio (more available customization than Express). Click the choice appropriate for your purposes.

How can I use Express?
Step 1: In the left column, you can choose already-created presentations that use media from news, entertainment, and other sources.

Step 2: In the middle column, you can choose from a variety of styles to house your presentation.

Step 3: In the right column, you can choose among variations within each style.

Step 4: All of your choices will appear in the frame to the right. After making your choices, click in the text box below your presentation to type in the title of your presentation.

Step 5: Click I'm Done.

Step 6: This will save your presentation in a presentation page, where you can share your presentation. Your sharing options are on the left-hand side: a link to share, send via e-mail, or embed your presentation in a website.

How can I use Collage?

Step 1: The main page allows you to explore already made collages and tutorial videos. To begin your own, click Create a New Collage at the top right corner of the page.

Step 2: A canvas will appear. You can choose to upload your own files and organize it yourself or use an automatic fill-in for files you upload. After using this site, you can also organize your files that you have previously uploaded, using the menu below your collage.

Step 3: Once files are uploaded, they will appear under the My Media tab at the bottom of the page. Click and drag your files onto the canvas.

Step 4: Once an image is in your collage, you can edit it. To move it, click and drag the image around your canvas.

Step 5: To resize your image, click the Double Arrow icon at the bottom right of the image and drag to the desired size.

Step 6: To draw a transparent area within the image, click the Scissors icon below the image. A new dialog box will appear. Specify the shape of the transparent area. When finished, click Done.

Step 7: To designate an image as a hot spot to which you can add a description or insert a slide show, click the Thought Bubble icon below the image. A bubble will appear. You can title the hot spot and add other media. Click outside the bubble to save the information.

Step 8: When two images are on top of each other, use the arrow icons at the right of the images to move one in front of or behind the other.

Step 9: To delete the image, click the red X at the top left corner of the image.

Step 10: To change the title of your collage, click Untitled Collage at the top left corner of the page. A box will appear. Type in a title and description for your collage. When finished, click OK.

Step 11: To add text to your collage, click the A icon at the top right corner of the page. A box will appear. Type in your text and change the color, font, and style as desired. To insert text into the collage, click and drag the text box from the right pane into your collage. The text box can also be moved around and resized in the same way as an image is (Steps 4 and 5 above).

Step 12: To add music to your collage, click the Music Note icon at the top right corner of the page. You can upload music files and determine how the tracks play (e.g., shuffle, loop, etc.).

Step 13: To preview your collage, click Preview at the top right corner of the page.

Step 14: To save your collage, click Save at the top right corner of the page.

Step 15: To publish your collage, click Publish at the top right corner of the page. A pane will appear on the right. Designate your collage as public or save as a draft by clicking the appropriate choice. Then click OK.

Step 16: A page will appear that allows you to choose whether to share your collage via Facebook, a URL embedded in a site, or an e-mail to others.

How can I use Studio?

Step 1: After clicking on Studio, a dialog box will open with a description of the program. Click Get Me Started.

Step 2: The next dialog box gives you options for uploading your images. Click the appropriate choice and click OK.

Step 3: Your canvas will appear with a tab at the top labeled Upload. Click this tab.

Step 4: A dialog box will appear to confirm the upload method you chose. Click Select Files From.

Step 5: Follow the directions to upload the images via the method you chose.

Step 6: After uploading your images, the dialog box you used to select your upload method will appear again. You can look for more images or minimize the box to begin your presentation.

Step 7: Your images will appear on the main screen. To add an image to your presentation, click and drag it to the column on the right side of the page.

Step 8: Continue moving as many images as you want in your presentation to the column on the right.

Step 9: To move images around in the column, click and drag them.

Step 10: To delete an image from the column (but not from your uploaded images), click the X at the top right corner of the image within the column.

Step 11: When you have moved all of the images over, click Create at the bottom right corner of the page.

Step 12: A dialog box will appear with a description of the next step, picking a style. Click OK.

Step 13: The tab at the top of the screen labeled Styles will be open. You can browse the available styles to create your presentation. Click on a presentation style that you like and it will appear on the canvas below.

Step 14: To resize or move an image within the presentation, click the Edit icon on the vertical toolbar to the left of the presentation. Click and drag your images to move or resize them.

Step 15: To add text to your presentation, click the Text icon on the vertical toolbar. A text box will appear for you to type in a caption, title, or other text.

Step 16: To add music to your presentation, click the Music icon on the vertical toolbar. A dialog box will appear that will allow you to upload music from the Internet or your computer.

Step 17: To add a frame to your presentation, click the Frame icon on the vertical toolbar. A dialog box will appear. Browse the available frames, then select your favorite to use in your project.

Step 18: To add a background to your presentation, click the Background icon on the vertical toolbar. A dialog box will appear. Browse the available backgrounds, then select your favorite to use in your project.

NOTE: Not all of these editing tools are available for every style.

Step 19: When finished with your presentation, click Save and Publish at the bottom right corner of the page.

Step 20: A new page will appear. Here, you can add a title and description to your presentation. You can also choose to send an e-mail of your presentation to others. Click Save.

Step 21: A new page will appear confirming that your presentation was published. You have the options of copying the code to embed your presentation into a website, editing the presentation, or creating a new presentation.

quikmaps

Description
quikmaps allows you to edit Google maps and personalize them for a variety of uses.

Resources
http://quikmaps.com/

How to begin?

Step 1: To create your own free account, click on Sign Up at the left side of the page.

Step 2: enter the corresponding information into the boxes and click Sign Up.

Step 3: Click Create New Map.

Step 4: A generic map will appear. Type in the address that you want to find into the box at the top of the page next to Go To. Click Go.

Step 5: The map of your location will appear.

How can I edit my map?

Step 1: You can change what your map looks like by choosing Map, Satellite, Hybrid, or Terrain at the top right corner of the map.

Step 2: To add a marker at a specific address or point on your map, click the marker from the menu on the right side of the page and drag it to where you want it. You can use markers, stars, and arrows to identify a variety of things on your map.

Step 3: To add text, click and drag the icon for Text Label from the menu to your map. A text box will appear wherever you put the icon. This allows you to label the markers on your map. When you are finished typing your text, click OK and the label will appear on your map.

Step 4: To add lines or routes to your map, click on Scribble above your map.

Step 5: To change the color of your line, click Pick. A dialog box will appear. Choose a color from the palette.

Step 6: Click and drag to draw a line on your map.

Step 7: You can insert a title and description for your map on the right side of the page.

Step 8: To save your map, click Save It at the bottom right corner of the page.

Step 9: To clear your map, click Clear on the right side of the page.

Step 10: To import another quikmap or file, click Import at the top right corner of the page. You can browse your computer or insert a website address to import a file.

Step 11: To change the background of your map, click Canvas at the top right corner of the page. You can choose Earth, Moon, Mars, or Sky.

TargetMap

Description
TargetMap allows you to create and share your own data maps using Google Maps.

Resources
http://www.targetmap.com/

How to begin?
Step 1: To begin, click Create Your Own Map.

Step 2: A new page will appear. You can choose whether or not to share your maps. Click on the appropriate choice for you.

Step 3: A new page will appear. Set up your free account by filling in the corresponding information, and then click Join.

Step 4: The next page will offer a video guide to creating your maps.

Step 5: The site will also send you an e-mail asking you click on a link to confirm your account.

How can I create my map?
Step 1: Clicking on the link sent to your e-mail will bring you to a blank world map. A dialog box will also appear on the left side. Choose the continent and country you want. Click Next.

Step 2: The next dialog box will allow you to choose how to insert your data. You can upload data from an Excel spreadsheet, type it in, or paint parts of the map. Click on the appropriate choice.

Step 3: A video will appear that shows you how to create your map using the selected method.

How can I share my map?
Step 1: Click Save at the bottom right corner of the dialog box.

Step 2: Type in the information for your map (e.g., title, description, source, etc.) and choose which type of information you are presenting, such as population or political preferences.

Step 3: Click Save.

Step 4: Click Share at the bottom right corner of the dialog box.

Step 5: Another dialog box will appear stating that you successfully saved your map. You can always edit again before sharing your map.

Step 6: Make any necessary edits and click Share. This publishes your map.

Step 7: Your first map must be reviewed by ReportMap to ensure quality. Within twenty-four hours, you will receive an e-mail regarding your map. If your first map is approved, then all later maps that you create will not need to be reviewed.

ChartGizmo

Description
ChartGizmo allows you to create charts to present information on a website, blog, or other online resource.

Resources
http://chartgizmo.com/

How to begin?
Step 1: Click the Create Account icon on the top right of the page.

Step 2: Enter a username and password to create an account. Click Signup.

Step 3: To create a chart, click New Chart.

How can I design and change the look of my chart?
Step 1: The Chart Editor page provides numerous options to choose from. Next to Chart Type, click the arrow on the right side of the box to see your choices. Click the appropriate option for your chart.

Step 2: You can use the boxes Chart Title, Comment, X Axis Label, and Y Axis Label to add text and descriptions to your chart.

Step 3: By clicking in the box next to Background Color and/or Plot Color, you can choose the color scheme for your chart.

Step 4: By clicking in the box next to Plot Orientation and/or Label Orientation, you can change the direction of the data plots in your chart or the labels on that data.

Step 5: You can also choose whether or not to show the legend or the data labels by choosing Show or Hide in the boxes next to the words Legend and/or Item Labels.

Step 6: A preview is shown on the right side of the page. After each change, you can click Update Preview under the preview picture to update the preview with the change(s).

How can I add data to create my chart?
Step 1: If you have data in an Excel spreadsheet, click the Import icon next to Source Data.

Step 2: A dialog box will appear. Copy and paste your data from Excel into the box provided. Click Import Data.

Step 3: If you do not have data in an Excel spreadsheet, you can enter it in the boxes provided under Source Data.

Step 4: To add a column of data, click the plus (+) sign next to Values.

Step 5: To add a row of data, click the farthest-right plus (+) sign next to Values.

Step 6: To add labels for your data, click in the boxes under Labels and type in the corresponding labels for each row of data.

Step 7: When you have finished adding data, click Save Chart.

How can I share my chart?

Step 1: Click Save and Publish after entering all of the information and data for your chart.

Step 2: The Chart Publishing page provides several methods to publish your chart, such as creating a link, an image, or code to enter it into a website. Click on the appropriate option.

Step 3: A box will appear under the title of the option you chose. Follow the directions in the box to share your chart in the manner you chose (e.g., Under Link to Chart is a link you can copy and paste to share your chart via a hyperlink).

Solvr

Description

Solvr assists you in solving problems collaboratively.

Resources

http://a.freshbrain.com/solvr//

How to begin?

Step 1: To begin, type in your problem in the box under What's Your Problem?

Step 2: Click Start.

Step 3: A new page will appear with your problem listed at the top.

Step 4: To add something to this problem, click Add Entry.

Step 5: A line will appear with two boxes. In the Fix box, you can choose whether your entry is an idea, comment, or additional problem related to the original problem.

Step 6: In the second box, type in the added idea, comment, or problem.

Step 7: Click Save or hit Enter on your keyboard. Your added idea, comment, or problem will appear under the original problem.

Step 8: You can repeat Steps 4–7 to add more ideas, comments, and problems.

Step 9: To edit or change any entry, click Edit to the right of the entry and change the text.

Step 10: To delete an entry, click the red X to the right of the entry.

Step 11: To add a separate problem to the same Solvr page, click Add Entry at the top of the page above the original problem statement.

Step 12: Type the new problem into the text box and click Save.

How can I share my Solvr problem and get feedback from others?

Step 1: To share your problem, copy and paste the URL found at the top of the page, above your problem. You can e-mail the URL to others or insert into a website or other media.

Step 2: Others will be able to view your problem and share their opinions.

Step 3: To vote for a particular entry, click Star to the right of the entry. A tally will appear (X votes) next to the star so that you can see how many votes each entry has received.

DecideAlready

Description

DecideAlready assists you in making group decisions, using an online survey program.

Resources

https://decidealready.com/

How to begin?

Step 1: Click Signup at the top right corner of the page.

Step 2: Enter the appropriate information into the corresponding boxes. (You will have the choice to pay to upgrade to a premium plan, but the standard plan is free).

Step 3: Click in the box at the bottom of the page to agree to the terms of service and click Signup.

Step 4: To start making a decision, type your question in the box under What Are You Deciding Today?

Step 5: Click Start Deciding.

Step 6: To add a possible answer, type in one answer under Add an Answer on the right side of the page.

Step 7: You may also add details in your answer for clarification by clicking Enter Answer Details and typing in the box that appears.

Step 8: When finished with the answer, click Add. Your answer choice will appear on the left side of the page under Your Proposed Answers.

Step 9: Repeat Steps 3–5 for all possible answers. You can also edit and delete answer choices as you go by clicking on Edit or Delete next to each answer option.

Step 10: When finished with entering all possible answers, click Next.

Step 11: You now have the option to add criteria for your answers, such as liking one answer more or less than another. To add a criterion, type it in the box under Add Criteria on the right side of the page.

Step 12: You may add details to clarify your criteria by clicking Enter Criterion Details and typing in the box that appears.

Step 13: When finished with a criterion, click Add. Your criterion will appear on the left side of the page under Your Criteria.

Step 14: Repeat Steps 8–10 for all criteria. You can also edit and delete criteria as you go by clicking on Edit or Delete next to each criterion.

Step 15: When finished entering all criteria, click Next.

How can I ask people to answer my question?

Step 1: To add participants to answer your question, enter their e-mail addresses in the box under Add Participants. (You can also import contacts if you create a free DecideAlready account).

Step 2: After entering your contacts' e-mail addresses, click Add Participants. A list of participants will appear on the left side of the page under Current Participants.

Step 3: When finished entering all participants, click Next.

What options do I have in how people answer my question?

Step 1: You can choose a deadline by entering a date and time under Response Deadline. (This is required to send out your question).

Step 2: To automatically publish the results when the deadline passes, click the box under the date and time you selected.

Step 3: You can also choose how participants answer your question by choosing Simple (pick one answer) or Ranked (rank answers in order of preference).

Step 4: When finished choosing options, click Next.

How do I send out my question?

Step 1: The next page will ask you to confirm your question, answers, criteria, and options. You can also add a personalized message to the e-mail that will be sent to your participants.

Step 2: To change something, click Edit next to the corresponding section title.

Step 3: When everything is the way that you want it, click Confirm. The website will send the question out to the participants automatically.

Step 4: The next page is an overview of your question and the page you will come back to in order to check on the progress of your decision.

How can I check on my question?

Step 1: After logging in, all of the questions you have sent will appear on the left side of the page under Questions I've Asked. Under the title is the date that the question was sent out and how many responses you have gotten so far.

Step 2: For more details, click the question that you would like to check on.

Step 3: An overview page will appear which is the page that you ended up on after sending out your question (see Step 4 under "How do I sent out my question?" above).

Step 4: You can add participants by clicking Add in the Participants box at the lower right corner of the page.

Step 5: You can also send a reminder to participants who have not responded by clicking Send Reminder under the specific participant's name.

Diffen

Description
Diffen allows you to compare and contrast any two things.

Resources
http://www.diffen.com/

How to begin?

Step 1: To compare two things, enter one item into each of the boxes in the middle of the page. (Examples and recently searched topics are listed on the bottom of the page.)

Step 2: Click Get Difference.

Step 3: A page will appear displaying a table. The two things that you searched for will be at the top of two columns. The farthest-left column will show a label for the attributes being compared under each item. If there is already information on the website, the table will be populated with information for each item.

Step 4: If there is not information already entered (or you would like to add something), click Edit Comparison Table at the top right above the table to add attributes.

Step 5: The table format will change and you will be able to add and delete attributes.

Step 6: To add attributes, click Add Attributes in the last row of the table. A blank row will appear, into which you can type additional attributes for each item.

Step 7: To delete attributes, click Delete at the right side of the row that you would like to delete.

Step 8: After making your changes, click Store Changes at the bottom of the page. (You can also click Cancel to ignore the changes and return to the original table.)

How do I compare and contrast the two items that I chose?

Step 1: To compare the items, click the icon next to Similarities above the table. All of the attributes that are similar between the two items will appear.

Step 2: To contrast the items, click the icon next to Differences above the table. All of the attributes that are different between the two items will appear.

Step 3: To see all of the attributes again for each item, click the icon next to All Attributes above the table.

Bubbl.us

Description
Bubbl.us allows you to create free, online mind maps to use for brainstorming ideas.

Resources
https://bubbl.us/

How to begin?
Step 1: Click on Create Account from the menu on the right-hand side of the page.

Step 2: Type in the corresponding information and click Create Account.

Step 3: Your username and password will be populated under Sign In on the right side of the page. Click Sign In.

Step 4: A Tip of the Day will appear in the center of your screen. Feel free to click Next (top right corner of box) to read through some of the tips to create mind maps. When finished, click Start Brainstorming.

How can I add text to make a mind map?
Step 1: A bubble will appear in the center of your screen that will serve as the center of your mind map. To type in text, click where it says Start Here.

Step 2: By putting your cursor over the bubble, options will appear that allow you to change the font and size of your text, connect one bubble to another, delete the bubble, or move the box to another place on the page.

Step 3: When you have finished with the center bubble, you have two options to create another bubble by putting your cursor over the center bubble: (1) To create a bubble connected to the center bubble (a "child bubble"), click the icon on the bottom ; OR (2) To create a bubble that is not connected to the center bubble, click the icon on the right.

Step 4: You may type in the new bubble just as you did with the original bubble.

Step 5: To create a new bubble from a connecting bubble, you have two options. Place your cursor over the connecting bubble, then: (1) To create a bubble that is at the same level as this bubble and connected to the center bubble (a "sibling bubble"), click the icon on the right; OR (2) To create a bubble that is connected to this bubble (a "child bubble), click the icon on the bottom.

Step 6: Repeat the above steps as needed until you have the bubbles you want formatted the way you want them.

How can I change and organize my mind maps?

Step 1: To change the size of your mind map, slide the zoom button (top left of page) to the desired size. You can also use the plus (+) sign to increase the size of the map or the minus (–) sign to decrease the size. The Fit icon will resize your mind map to fill the entire page.

Step 2: The remaining icons at the top left of the page allow you to undo the last change you made, copy and paste items, and print your mind map. The Export icon allows you to save the mind map in a different format, such as JPEG.

Step 3: To save, click the Save icon at the top right of the page. The arrow to the right of the icon allows you to Save As and create a new copy of the mind map.

Step 4: To create a fresh page, click the Sheet icon at the far right of the page under Sheets.

Step 5: To create a new folder for your mind maps, click the Folder icon on the far right of the page under Sheets. You can rename the folder and save mind maps into this folder to keep them organized.

Step 6: To enlarge the mind map page to full screen (the column on the right side of the page will disappear), click the arrow ("toggle") icon at the top right of the mind map page, above the Save icon.

How can I share my mind maps?

Step 1: To create a contact to share your mind maps with, click Contacts on the right side of the page. The will open the Contacts window.

Step 2: To create a contact, click Add Contacts.

Step 3: An Add Contacts dialog box will appear. Enter a name, e-mail, or Bubbl.us username to search for contacts. (Your contacts must also have a Bubbl.us account in order to share your mind maps.)

Step 4: Click the desired contact and click Add to Contacts.

Step 5: To organize your contacts into groups, click the Groups icon to create a folder within your contacts. You can rename the folder to organize your contacts.

Step 6: To delete a contact, click on the contact name in the Contacts box and then click Delete at the bottom right of the Contacts box.

Step 7: To share your mind maps, click the Sharing icon at the top right of the page under Sheets.

Step 8: A Sharing Permissions dialog box will appear. In the left column, click on the sheets or mind maps that you would like to share. In the right column, click on the contact(s) with whom you would like to share the selected sheets. Click Apply Permissions and Close.

Step 9: You can also chat with your contacts if they are online at the same time. To chat with a contact, click the Chat icon (it looks like a speech bubble) at the top right corner of the Contacts box.

Bookr

Description
Bookr allows you to create an online photobook using Flickr images.

Resources
http://www.pimpampum.net/bookr/

How to begin?
Step 1: Click in the box displaying the words "Write a title for your photobook" and type in a title.

Step 2: Click in the box with the word Author and type in the name of the author.

Step 3: To create a new page, click the Add (+) icon at the bottom right side of the photobook.

Step 4: Use the remaining icons at the bottom right side of the photobook to move to different pages. (The top right box of the group goes to the first page; the bottom left box goes to the last page.)

How can I add text, images, etc.?
Step 1: To search for images, click in the box at the bottom of the page next to Tag.

Step 2: Type in a search term and Flickr images will populate in a horizontal panel along the bottom of the page.

Step 3: Click on and drag the image that you want to the appropriate page. The image will upload to fill almost the entire page.

Step 4: To add a caption to the image, click in the rectangle at the bottom and type in the caption.

Step 5: To delete an image, click Delete Image located at the top of each image.

Step 6: When finished with the photobook, click on Publish This Book at the bottom right of the page. The photobook is now saved in your account.

How do I share my photobook?
Step 1: To send your photobook via e-mail, click in the box next to Send To: at the bottom left of the page.

Step 2: Insert e-mail address(es) and click Go to share your photobook.

Step 3: At the bottom right-hand side of the page, there are other options to create a new photobook, recycle (use the current photobook to create a new one), blog the photobook (share it using a website), or view archives (previously created photobooks).

Step 4: To insert your photobook into a blog or other website, click on Blog This at the bottom right of the page.

Step 5: You can choose between publishing an image of the cover page of the photobook or a link of the title of the photobook. Text is provided to copy and paste in the website where you are sharing your photobook.

Penzu

Description

Penzu allows you to create a journal to record thoughts, plans, etc. as if writing on a pad of paper.

Resources

http://penzu.com/

How to begin?

Step 1: Click Create Your Free Journal to create a free account.

Step 2: Enter the appropriate information (e.g., name, username, password), click the box for "I agree to the terms …," and then click Submit.

Step 3: Once logged in, you will be able to customize your journal and sync your account to other accounts you may have, such as Twitter or Facebook. Select the choices you want and click Next through each of these options, until you come to your journal.

Step 4: To enter your journal, click on [Name]'s Journal. This will open a "pad" where you can type.

Step 5: Begin typing on the pad where it says Enter Title and Begin Typing Here.

Step 6: To save your journal entry, click on the Save icon above the pad (the second icon from the left). To print your journal, click on the Printer icon above the pad (the third icon from the left).

Step 7: To create a new journal entry, click on the New icon above the pad (the first on the left).

Step 8: To view previous entries, click the icon that looks like several sheets of paper on the right-hand side of the page. A box will appear with recent journal entries. Click on the entry that you want.

How do I add text, images, etc?

Step 1: To insert images, click the camera icon above the pad (the fourth icon from the left). You will be able to upload photos within each entry.

Step 2: You have the option to upload images from your computer or your Flickr account. Click Go under the appropriate option.

Step 3: To upload images from your computer, click Browse Computer and an Open dialog box will appear. Go through your computer files to find the image that you would like to add.

Step 4: Click on the image name and click Open.

Step 5: The image will appear in the Upload From Computer box in your journal. You may then upload another image if you choose.

Step 6: When you have finished uploading all of your images, click Done. The image(s) will appear in a box above the pad.

Step 7: To attach the image(s) to the journal entry, click Attach at the top of the image(s). (You can insert images directly into the text of the entry if you subscribe to the Pro version of Penzu).

How do I share a journal entry?

Step 1: Click the Share icon above the pad (fifth icon from the left).

Step 2: A dialog box will appear. Enter an e-mail address and a personal message to share your journal entry.

How do I lock a journal entry so that no one else can view it?

Step 1: Click the Lock icon above the pad (fifth icon from the right).

Step 2: A dialog box will appear. Enter your password (twice) and include a password hint. (You will be asked to enter this password each time you access this journal entry).

Masher

Description
Masher allows you to create videos using various other media, such as photos, videos, and music.

Resources
http://www.masher.com/

How to begin?
Step 1: On the main page, click Get Started in the bottom right corner.

Step 2: Fill in the corresponding information to sign up for your free account, and click Submit.

Step 3: A screen will appear confirming that you have registered your account. Click Click Here to Login.

Step 4: Enter your username and password and click Login.

Step 5: This will bring you to your main page where all your "Mashes" will be held.

How can I create a Mash?
Step 1: From your main page, click on Studio in the top right corner.

Step 2: You can use videos that are already included in the site. To insert a video into your Mash, click and drag the video clip from the menu on the right to the timeline below next to Videos/Photos.

Step 3: You can browse the available videos by clicking on Videos at the top, where different menus will appear. Click on the different menus to look through the videos.

Step 4: To upload your own video, click My Uploads. You can choose to upload videos, photos, or music.

Step 5: Click on what you would like to upload. A screen will appear that allows you to browse your computer and select the media that you want to insert into your Mash.

Step 6: To add music to your Mash, click on Music at the top and a list of menus will appear. From these, you can choose music from different genres.

Step 7: Click and drag the song that you want into the timeline at the bottom next to Music.

Step 8: To delete a video or music clip from your Mash, put your cursor over the video or music clip in the timeline. A red X will appear at the top right of the video or music clip box. Click the X.

Step 9: To save your Mash, click Save in the bottom right. A dialog box will appear. Insert a title, description, and tags for your Mash then click save.

Integration Ideas

One of the problems with classroom technology integration is that teachers often focus on the technology aspect. When designing a traditional unit or lesson, teachers rarely stop with simple information gathering. They ask students to compare and contrast, synthesize, or apply the information. Why would we then not expect them to do the same with technology? In much the same way, good teachers rarely use only one method of teaching a concept. Instead, they teach it in a variety of ways to reach all learning types in their classes. Technology should be used in the same manner.

(Beaver and Moore)

Now that you have read the various professional development plans, read through the tutorials, and are probably starting to form some concepts as to how you are going to use this information, it is time to make sure we understand a bit about how to integrate technology into the classroom and how to associate instructional technology with proven educational platforms.

Administrator/Staff Tech Tools

The tech tools in this next section have been chosen to help save time, manage and organize, research, and communicate more efficiently. These tools can be used as instructional tools or as managerial tools for teachers and administrators. In each of the Pro Dev Plans teachers are asked to share several of these tools. You can pick freely from the lists below; however, it is suggested that you choose one from each category for each Pro Dev day.

BLOOM'S TAXONOMY

EVALUATION

SYNTHESIS

ANALYSIS

APPLICATION

COMPREHENSION

KNOWLEDGE

Bloom's Taxonomy has been around for ages and should not be anything new to even the most novice educator (Krathwohl 215). During the 1990s, researchers updated the traditional terms in Bloom's Taxonomy to reflect twenty-first century learning and the use of technology in that new learning system. The words in green are the updated terms that are now accepted as the new Bloom's Taxonomy (Krathwohl 215). Notice how the words go from nouns to verbs. There is a need for action in education, and the verbs support that thinking. One of the most exciting changes is the use of the word "creating." Technology has been the reason for many of these changes.

The instructional E-Tools shared in this publication each fit in multiple sections of the taxonomy. You can see that the use of E-Tools makes it much easier for our students to work on the higher-order thinking skills in the new Bloom's Taxonomy. It is not uncommon for teachers to struggle to reach those higher levels, but with the use of E-Tools, it becomes simple.

BLOOM'S TAXONOMY

CREATING

EVALUATION

EVALUATING

SYNTHESIS

ANALYZING

ANALYSIS

APPLYING

APPLICATION

UNDERSTANDING

COMPREHENSION

REMEMBERING

KNOWLEDGE

The location of a given E-Tool in the new Bloom's Taxonomy will depend greatly on how the teacher decides to use the E-Tool.

1. *Creating/Evaluating*: All the tools considered in this level of learning allow students to create new products.

2. *Evaluating/Synthesis*: All tools considered in this level of learning allow students to debate and justify a position on a topic.

3. *Analyzing/Analysis*: All tools considered in this level of learning allow students to distinguish between different elements through compare/contrast and to examine what has been taught.

4. *Applying/Application*: All tools allow students to use information in a new way. They can choose a concept and illustrate or dramatize it in order to make it real to them.

5. *Understanding/Comprehension*: All tools considered in this level of learning allow students to explain ideas and concepts through discussion and description.

6. *Remembering/Knowledge*: All tools considered in this level of learning allow students to recall, repeat, and/or use new information.

BLOOM'S TAXONOMY

CREATING

Glogster VUVOX
GoAnimate

EVALUATING

Museum Box Webspiration
quickmaps Hot Potatoes
DecideAlready

ANALYZING

Prezi TargetMaps Diffen
Hot Potatoes ChartGizmo
Museum Box Webspiration

APPLYING

GoAnimate VUVOX Masher
Hot Potatoes Penzu
Solvr

UNDERSTANDING

Bubbl.us Prezi
Bookr DecideAlready

REMEMBERING

Glogster WebQuest
Webspiration Bookr

Like Bloom's Taxonomy, using E-Tools will help you associate your instructional technology with Gardner's Multiple Intelligences (Armstrong). By using the graph "Multimedia Tools in Gardner's Multiple Intelligences" below, you can quickly and easily choose which E-Tool to assign your students based on their strengths and weaknesses.

1. *Linguistic*: All tools considered under this intelligence provide opportunities for the learner to expand on new learning through writing, reflection, and explanation of what was learned or taught.

2. *Logical*: All tools considered under this intelligence provide opportunities for the learner to create abstract representations of material using data and charts.

3. *Interpersonal*: All tools considered under this intelligence provide opportunities for the learner to apply new learning in a group or social setting

4. *Intrapersonal*: All tools considered under this intelligence provide opportunities for the learner to internalize material.

5. *Kinesthetic*: All tools considered under this intelligence provide opportunities for the learner to have hands-on and active experiences with curriculum concepts.

6. *Visual/Spatial*: All tools considered under this intelligence provide opportunities for the learner to have experiences in which they can visualize and manipulate objects,

7. *Auditory*: All tools considered under this intelligence provide opportunities for the learner to create or have an experience using music.

Multimedia Tools in Gardner's Multiple Intelligences							
Linguistic: Word Smart	Logical: Number Smart	Interpersonal: People Smart	Intrapersonal:	Kinesthetic: Body/hands-on	Naturalistic: Nature/natural	Visual/Spatial: Picture Smart	Auditory: Music/musical
Penzu Bookr Hot Potatoes	Bubbl.us TargetMap ChartGizmo	Glogster Prezi Diffen	Museum Box WebQuest Penzu Webspiration	quikmaps GoAnimate Masher		quikmaps GoAnimate Glogster VUVOX	Masher Wetoku

If we also take a look at the common acceptable standards for twenty-first century learning as offered on its website by the American Association of School Librarians, you once again can see how using these E-Tools in the classroom will be a benefit to your students. You can use the table to choose E-Tools that complement the needs of your classroom.

Inquire, think critically, and gain knowledge.	
	Penzu Bookr Hot Potatoes Bubbl.us TargetMap
Draw conclusions, make informed decisions, apply knowledge to new situations, and create new knowledge.	
	TargetMap ChartGizmo Glogster Prezi Diffen Masher Wetoku
Share knowledge and participate ethically and productively as members of our democratic society.	
	quikmaps GoAnimate Glogster VUVOX Museum Box
Pursue personal and aesthetic growth.	
	WebQuest Penzu Webspiration

Integration is one of the key elements for infusing technology into the classroom. The understanding of how E-Tools will enrich and enhance learning for the student will also make this professional development plan a more worthwhile experience for the teachers.

Management E-Tools

This next section shares many E-Tools that can be used to lighten the daily workload of teachers and administrators. Not only can E-Tools help in the classroom, but we can also use them to ease the time management crunch that we all experience each day. These E-Tools can be used to help organize your workload, research important new trends in education, or communicate more efficiently with your staff or other educators. By using these E-Tools, you will not only be helping yourself, but also be modeling good use of technology for your teachers and staff. Most, if not all, of these E-Tools are free. They are typically very easy to learn and use on a regular basis.

The management E-Tools have been categorized as follows :

Collaboration Tools

Organization and Management Tools

Research Tools

Communication Tools

In the professional development plans described earlier in this book, you were requested to choose at least two management E-Tools to share with your staff. Choose whichever tools that you see would be of the greatest benefit to you and/or your staff.

Collaboration Tools

Teamwork is the ability to work together toward a common vision; the ability to direct individual accomplishment toward organizational objectives. It is the fuel that allows common people to attain uncommon results.

—*Andrew Carnegie (*Khurana*)*

Collaboration is one of the most powerful tools that a leader has. When the stakeholders involved work together to solve a problem systematically, not only does the process become an effective way to develop focus and form solutions, but those who are collaborating also become invested in making the emerging plan successful. Collaboration can occur among staff members, parents, and community stakeholders. Student collaboration is also a useful method for enhancing student engagement in learning.

The term "collaborative leadership" began to appear in literature regarding the private sector in the mid-90s (Hopkins). Jim Collins, author of *Good to Great*, provides empirical evidence that collaborative, mission-driven strategies are essential within companies. His concept of "independent, collaborative companies within companies" transfers logically to schools where collaborative teams work within the larger school entity ("Good").

"Increasingly, great accomplishments happen when people collaborate; that means that the new job of leaders is to guide those collaborations" (Ibarra and Hansen). Unfortunately a fifteen-year study by Herminia Ibarra and Morten Hansen showed that, while collaboration requires collaborative leadership, only 16% of leaders in the study demonstrated that kind of leadership.

These researchers suggest that the collaborative leader needs to be well versed in the following skill sets:

1. Connector Roles: spot opportunities to embrace and encourage collaboration— connect people to opportunities. Share power and influence.

2. Diverse Talents: harness diversity of knowledge, resources, and perspectives. Create teams made up of diverse people with varying and even polarized ideas. Bring out the best in everyone by developing individual talents.

3. Dynamic Networks: enable teamwork by creating the right context for it to flourish— disciplined flexibility.

4. Learning Mindsets: build relationships that value long-term learning. (Ibarra and Hansen)

Elements of collaboration have been successfully practiced in schools for decades, particularly among teachers who have been involved in team teaching. As we face the future, it will be even more important for students to learn to collaborate. Collaboration and communication, always an imperative part of team endeavors, are identified as important twenty-first century skills. Current and emerging technologies will make it possible for this kind of collaboration to take place beyond the walls of the classroom with greater efficiency and effectiveness.

The following section provides a list of E-Tools that will aid in the development of collaboration and communication among your staff and/or students.

Google Docs

http://www.docs.google.com

Google has many E-Tools that will be discussed throughout this handbook. The first one is Google Docs. This is a fully collaborative, Microsoft Office-style workstation. You can create a text document, presentation, or spreadsheet. The uniqueness of this workstation is that you can share these documents with anyone who has an Internet connection. They can work right along with you on any given document ... even at the same time. Google Docs saves the work every few seconds, and revisions are kept in a history section.

School Benefits

- Collaboration with colleagues from any distance.

- Intradistrict collaboration, such as the district handbook or the district budget. Several colleagues can work on the same document at the same time from any distance.

- No worries about returning the drafts and compiling the drafts from various people into one master document.

- It is simple to invite other people to view your document with an attached URL for each document. Sending documents is easy, and you know that you are sending the correct draft.

- Sharing documents such as volunteer lists between the office and PTO/booster organizations is simple and easy to update between organizations.

WizIQ

http://www.wiziq.com

This is a free virtual classroom. The features are simple but great for the cost. There is no software to download—everything is based right on the Internet. Distance learning, virtual meetings, and information sharing are just some of the uses of WizIQ.

School Benefits

- Free virtual classroom.

- Desktop and screen sharing.

- Share PowerPoint, Flash, PDF, and document files for group viewing.

- All sessions are recorded and downloadable for archiving.

- Great for parent workshops and teacher professional development.

- Can be used to create lessons that teachers must watch and verify, such as EpiPen usage, food allergy updates, etc.

JustPaste.it

http://justpaste.it/

This tool is useful for taking notes when you are on the go and don't have anywhere to save the information. Students can look at notes that the teacher has posted. Students can also take their own notes.

School Benefits

- Paste text and share with your friends.

- Quickest way to share text with other people.

- Automatic text backup.

- Never ever lose your notes because of a browser crash again.

Webs

http://www.webs.com

Webs is a free service for creating websites. You get just about every feature a website can offer. Your website can have a blog, members' area, forums, video files, photo albums, and more.

School Benefits

- Free Web presence.

- Many extra features for free.

- Use as a classroom supplement.

- Use for teacher in-service.

- Area for collaboration

Spruz

http://www.spruz.com

Spruz is more than just a Web presence. It is a social media site. You can use Spruz to create an entire social network dedicated to your topic of choice. It is as powerful as any website and as intricate as any social media site.

School Benefits

- Social site completely controlled by the owner.

- Teachers can collaborate with a sense of security.

- Free with a lot of web page space.

Premier Survey

https://www.premiersurvey.com/

This is a free survey creation and implementation site. You can create various kinds of questions and send out the survey via e-mail. Respondents will respond to the survey via the Internet. You can use a number of different charts to graph the results.

School Benefits

- Free survey system.

- Ability to manipulate the data in a variety of ways.

- Surveys are online; no need to use hard copies.

- Surveys are sent by e-mail.

Poll Everywhere

http://www.polleverywhere.com

This is another survey website with a twist. This site lets you create slides that can easily be added to presentations and websites. The participants answer the questions in a variety of ways. They can answer via Twitter, a website, or text using their cell phone, to name a few. The results are instantly displayed, giving you immediate feedback.

School Benefits

- Quickly gather staff responses to various questions at a staff meeting.

- Use the "fill up" version of the response template to track donations, books read, etc.

- Models good use of modeling technology in a professional development setting.

- Instant, real-time results of polls.

- A variety of media can be used to answer poll questions.

- Questions can be displayed via slides and results shown in real time.

GoAnimate4Schools

http://www.goanimate4schools.com/pubic_index

This website is a safe environment for students to fully express their creativity through animation, and a great place for educators to share their practices and experiences.

School Benefits

- State-of-the-art animation tools.

- Gets students to put learning to practice.

- Lesson Gallery is a growing database of educational material created by educators using GoAnimate, which can be used in your classroom.

- Most popular animations are literature, languages, math, and science.

Paper Critters

http://www.papercritters.com

This is a Flash Web application for creating and sharing digital paper toys and creating printable cartoon "people." You can choose the Toy Creator if you want to start making a toy or The Colony to view an interactive gallery of all the toys. Critters are all the same shape—a big-headed, blocky "person." Each character also gets a Flash embed code that links to a spinning 3-D model of the character.

School Benefits

- Provides a comprehensive editor with lots of "stamps" (eyes).

- Allows for freehand drawing.

- Design the sides and back of the figure as well.

SAM Animation

http://www.samanimation.com

This desktop application allows users to capture a series of still images from a webcam and play the images back in movie form. SAM, which stands for "stop-action-movies," was developed by Tufts University with support from the National Science Foundation. As of 2011, the software is exclusively licensed to http://www.icreatetoeducate.com/, a young company dedicated to giving students the tools to drive their own learning in the K-12 classroom.

School Benefits

- Creative Outlet.

- Designed specifically for students and teachers.

- Get video results without expensive video projectors and complicated video software.

Sharendipity

http://www.sharendipity.com

This is a fun and easy way to create social games or multimedia experiences and share them with your friends. Anyone can build and deploy engaging and interactive Web applications anywhere on the Web.

School Benefits

- K-12 learning tools.

- Free creation tools inside browser.

- Integrates third-party Web services.

- No programming required.

Scratch

http://www.scratch.mit.edu

You can imagine, program, and create your own interactive stories, games, music, and art on this site. Be a part of Scratch Day, which is a worldwide network of gatherings when "Scratchers" come together to meet, share, and learn. Check out new collections of intro video tutorials and find Scratch on various wiki websites.

School Benefits

- Interactive.

- Simple and student-friendly, so students can work on this alone.

- Highly creative and useful for challenging enrichment students.

Organization and Management

The secret of all victory lies in the organization of the non-obvious.
—Marcus Aurelius ("Marcus")

A school principal quickly discovers that the "urgent" often conflicts with the "important." This is largely due to the duality of the role of principal: manager and instructional leader. This is not to suggest that one role is more important than the other, for both are equally crucial and require the attention of the principal. However, most of the urgent demands on a principal's time and energies seem to be related to his/her role as manager. Finance, school law, scheduling, transportation, discipline, public relations, and food services must be managed, and they all fall on the shoulders of the principal. Time management and multitasking are profoundly important for the twenty-first century principal.

Throughout the history of public education in America, those entrusted with managing schools have been confronted with demands on their time and have responded by seeking new strategies to meet their obligations. It is critical that today's school administrator continues to seek new strategies for managing more efficiently, since new demands on their time are continually surfacing. Francis Bacon addressed this need when he stated, "He that will not apply new remedies must expect new evils; for time is the greatest innovator" (Bacon 280).

Education World's Principal Files Team shares, "Time management consultants agree that to effectively manage time, people must plan, delegate, organize, direct, and control" (Hopkins). Principals often say that as part of their time-management organizational plan, the school secretary takes on many responsibilities to help ease the load (Hopkins). Perhaps the use of appropriate technology might not only help organize the school principal, but also relieve the school secretary of some managerial responsibilities.

What follows are several E-Tools that the principal of today may find useful in fulfilling some of his/her managerial responsibilities.

Only2Clicks

http://www.only2clicks.com

This is the simplest and most useful of Web applications. Your entire bookmark collection is in one place. You can access it from a desktop, laptop, airport lounge, or iPhone. You can organize frequently visited websites in tabs. One tab could be for social bookmarks, one for online shops, and one for work. Think of it as a speed dial for your most used websites. Simply rearrange icons by dragging and dropping. Favorite search engines can also be gathered in one bookmark by creating new skins.

School Benefits

- Import bookmarks from other applications.

- Export bookmarks to another account for backup.

- Share links with friends.
- Interface with iPhone and iPod.

PictureTrail

http://www.picturetrail.com

This site offers the biggest slideshow selection on the Web! You can share photos, host images, and display camera-phone photos.

School Benefits

- Music for your albums.
- Custom album covers.
- Slideshow screensaver.
- Photo editor/uploader.

Classroom Architect

http://www.classroom.4teachers.org

For students, classroom environment is very important. The size of the classroom and interior areas, colors of walls, type of furniture and flooring, amount of light, and room arrangement all influence how students learn. Thoughtful arrangement of the indoor and outdoor environments will support your learning goals for students. This tool provides an opportunity for experimentation with the layout of your classroom without any heavy lifting!

School Benefits

- Select basic dimensions.
- Easily drag typical classroom items in to your project.
- Print out your classroom.

Gliffy

http://www.gliffy.com

Easily create great-looking diagrams for free. Diagrams include professional-quality flowcharts, floor plans, technical drawings and more.

School Benefits

- Network layouts.
- Venn diagrams.
- Organizational charts.
- Flow charts.
- SWOT charts.

Zoho Creator

http://www.zoho.com/creator

Zoho Creator is an easy-to-use platform that lets you build custom database applications such as library catalogs and assignment trackers on your own, online, in minutes.

School Benefits

- Data collection, analysis, reporting and collaboration.

- Online form, workflow and business rules, notifications.

- Design HTML views, brand with your logo and themes.

BonzoBox

http://www.bonzobox.com

This is a homepage that makes sharing websites and bookmarks with your colleagues or students fast and easy.

School Benefits

- Add up to thirty educational sites on home page.

- Teachers can create pages of bookmarks for their students based on a specific subject.

- Visually easy to see and find your sites.

stickybits

http://www.stickybits.com/

A smartphone app very similar to barcode or QR code scanners. It allows users to access embedded videos, links, audio, or online sites. The stickybits app also allows users to win prizes from barcodes or QR codes they scan. For example, Lipton has murals up around the country that users can scan in order to potentially win prizes. This app has great uses in the marketplace. Using it in the schools would be a more creative endeavor. Barcode or QR codes apps like stickybits have a place in the schools, but some obstacles still exist before they can be a positive and worthwhile venture for schools on a large scale.

School Benefits

- Codes can allow students to access assignments, notes, examples, and other curriculum information at any time via their smartphones, or send this information to their computers.

- Codes can be embedded in worksheets or tests to allow students to view a video or hear an audio clip in order to analyze and answer a question.

- Codes linking students to content may be placed around the building or in textbooks to bring a subject to life and provide a learning environment.

- Technology required for this application would be a smartphone with access to a barcode or QR code scanner, or a device that can play codes and send them to an alternate device. Such devices would need access to smartphone technology

Google Calendar

http://www.google.com/calendar

The Google calendar system is a simple calendar with the added benefit of being able to overlay other people's calendars onto your own. You can also give others the ability to manipulate your calendar.

School Benefits

- Secretary can alter your calendar from anywhere there is Internet access.

- You can check your calendar from any computer, including your cell phone (with a data service).

- Keeping various calendars such as home and school is a benefit. When you overlay the calendars, you can see free time and double bookings.

- The superintendent can keep an overlaid copy of all the administrators' calendars on his or her desktop and be able to schedule meetings based on the availability of all the administrators.

4shared

http://www.4shared.com

This is a file locker where you can store or share files of up to ten gigabytes. You can redownload the files anywhere you can get Internet access.

School Benefits

- Files can be retrieved from anywhere you have Internet access.

- Files can be retrieved by anyone who has the code to for that particular file.

- File storage up to ten gigabytes is free.

- No more need for flash drives and external hard drives.

HitMeLater

http://hitmelater.com

This is an e-mail address that you can use to forward your own e-mails. When you forward your e-mail to this address, it will resend the e-mail back to you within a set number of hours (up to twenty-four). For example, if you want the e-mail sent back to you in eight hours, you would send it to 8@hitmelater.com.

School Benefits

- Organizes your e-mail in-box.

- Gives you an opportunity to receive an e-mail again when you may have more time to deal with that e-mail.

- Organizes e-mails based on levels of importance and time-sensitivity.

HassleMe

http://www.hassleme.co.uk/

HassleMe is a simple and free reminder system that can be programmed to hassle you about anything. You set up the "hassle" with your e-mail address and choose the frequency with which you wish to be hassled. After that given duration of time, you will receive an e-mail that you wrote to yourself hassling you about your chosen topic.

School Benefits:

- Receive regular reminders about important events.

- Frequency can be altered for maximum or minimum amount of regular e-mails.

Guerrilla Mail

http://www.guerrillamail.com/

This is a free, temporary e-mail address that is totally anonymous. It only lasts for sixty minutes; then it disappears.

School Benefits:

- Anonymous.

- Great for battling spam.

- When you sign up for free trials that need authentication with an e-mail, use this service to keep your identity safe.

Infoencrypt

http://infoencrypt.com/

This is an online encryption tool. This is a great way to send confidential and secure information across the Internet. (Please note that although this website is functional, there are always risks. This site has not been updated for some time and new encryption protocols have since become a Web standard.) You write your message in the field and then choose a password. You send the message to another person who would know the password and who can then retrieve the message.

School Benefits

- Keeps e-mails confidential.

- Password-protects files sent through e-mail.

pdfforge.org

http://www.pdfforge.org/

This is a free, simple application that lets you save files in the PDF format. You will want to save all documents that go out to parents and other institutions in PDF format. PDF format is rarely modifiable. This keeps anyone from changing your document and sending out inaccurate information.

School Benefits

- Uses the standard PDF format.

- PDF forms are not modifiable.

- Everyone can open up a PDF file with a free mini-app on the Internet.

KeePass

http://keepass.info/

This tiny app lets you create a strong password and remembers to which app that password belongs. It is encrypted and also password protected, so you only need to remember one password even though you may have several varieties.

School Benefits

- Keeps all of your passwords in one convenient place.

- Lets you organize all of your passwords.

Launchy

http://www.launchy.net/

Launchy is an open-source keystroke launcher. Sometimes all of those icons on your desktop get messy and confusing. Launchy runs behind the scenes. All you have to do is type a few key letters or hit a predetermined button and your favorite applications will run.

School Benefits

- Keeps a clean and orderly desktop.

- Uses simple one- and two-button choices to open an application.

Pandora Recovery

http://www.pandorarecovery.com/

Pandora Recovery simply recovers anything that has accidentally been deleted, even after the trash has been dumped. This application will find your lost or trashed files.

School Benefits

- Anything that has been deleted from your hard drive is recoverable.

- Safeguards from accidental deletion.

DropSend

http://www.dropsend.com/

Most e-mail clients will not let you send very large files. Mainly you can send a few pictures and that's about it. With DropSend, you can send e-mail attachments of up to two gigabytes in size. This is becoming more and more important because files in general are becoming larger than they ever were in the past.

School Benefits

- Send files up to two gigabytes.

- Will not slow down your personal e-mail client.

Research

When fulfilling a leadership position in any organization, whether it's a company, school, or other group of people, one must have a thorough knowledge of research and how it can enhance one's leadership skills. Research is essential for informed decision making. For instance, research within an organization allows the leader to have a feel for how the organization is performing. A leader can utilize the research results to better understand his or her staff and the talent that is available. With the most relevant information available, the leader is better able to plan for the future. Furthermore, outside the organization, research helps the leader to acquire additional knowledge in his or her area of expertise and to present relevant information to staff. Overall, research saves money, time, and frustration.

Google Scholar

http://scholar.google.com/

This is a simple search engine. However, it only generates results from peer-reviewed, research-based material. This is the best search engine if you are looking to avoid all the clutter of a typical search and get right to the heart of peer-reviewed material.

School Benefits

- Search results are based on credible research.

- Educators can be confident that they are reading the most up-to-date research on search topics.

eHow

http://www.ehow.com/

eHow is an online how-to guide with more than one million articles and 170,000 videos offering step-by-step instructions. eHow content is created by both professional experts and amateur members and covers a wide variety of topics organized into different categories, thus making browsing easier.

School Benefits

- Can use and show different forms of media.

- Can reference the website and show teacher videos on different subject material.

Infoplease

http://www.infoplease.com/

Infoplease is an almanac, dictionary, encyclopedia, atlas, search engine, and teacher resource center all rolled into one. Infoplease offers the one-stop search and browsing that you cannot find for most topics. A sample search of China pulled up a map, country statistics, historical background, lesson examples, worksheets, and links to other websites. For some, this may be information overload, but for those of us who need bigger, better, and faster, Infoplease offers more than most people need.

School Benefits

- Results can be refined to look for a specific item.

- Teachers can build projects strictly around this site.

- Great introduction to Internet searching for a younger audience.

- Good training tool for proper Internet search methods.

- Many questions can be answered without leaving this one site.

- Great use for social studies, art, music, drama, and English language and literature curricula.

- Avoids nonacademic information produced by other search engines.

Policy Tool

http://socialmedia.policytool.net

This is a policy generator that simplifies the process of creating guidelines that respect the rights of your students and staff while also keeping your district safe.

School Benefits

- Easy to use.

- Requires you to answer a brief questionnaire.

- Provides you with a complete social media policy customized to your organization.

- Developed by leading authorities in Internet and technology-related legal issues.

Communication

Good leaders are good communicators. Leaders clearly communicate values and expectations for their organization. However, one must realize that clear communication is a two-way process. It's not enough to speak clearly; you have to make sure you're being heard and understood. Leaders must master numerous communication techniques in order to reach this goal. Leaders understand their audiences and are able to build a rapport with them, thus increasing the likelihood that the audience will act on what is being communicated.

Another key communication skill is to spend more time listening than talking. Do not finish the sentences of others, and do not answer questions with questions. Within any organization, little is accomplished without clear communication from the leader. Technology can be a positive force in the fight for clear and accurate communication.

Meetsee

http://meetsee.com/

Meetsee is a virtual office and meeting program that is designed to allow workers to communicate with office staff and other personnel to complete tasks even though they are not in the building. Administrators and teachers can communicate from home and hold meetings even when they are not together. Districts can conduct in-service programs from home and save money on building costs and trainings for that day. Teachers may also communicate directly with an administrator or another teacher without leaving the classroom, especially if a question arises in the middle of the day.

School Benefits

- Administrators and teachers can work from home or while away from building.

- Meetings can take place at any time.

- Programs and trainings can be offered at any time.

- Staff members can have their own virtual conversations.

- Small monthly fees ($70) are charged for groups under fifty members, and there are programs designed for small or large businesses with unlimited users (price varies).

ooVoo

http://www.oovoo.com

ooVoo is a free video conferencing site. There is a small application that you can download. The service provides basic face-to-face conferencing with video and audio support.

School Benefits

- Save time running from location to location for meetings.

- Audio and face-to-face conferencing.

- Distance learning.

VoiceThread

http://voicethread.com/

Group conversations can be collected and shared on this site from anywhere in the world, with no software to install. You can present collaborative, multimedia slideshows containing images, documents, and videos. Participants can navigate slides and leave comments five ways—using voice, text, audio file, or video via a webcam. Users can doodle while commenting and pick which comments are shown. Ed.VoiceThread, a secure and accountable environment found at ed.voicethread.com, is a Web-based communications network built specifically for K-12 students and educators.

School Benefits

- Best utilized in an upper-level (middle school or high school) setting.
- Use this program in everyday classrooms.
- Let students work autonomously.
- Available in school or out of school.
- Site is very secure and safe.

Dropbox

http://www.dropbox.com

Forget something? Plan ahead and put your files from your laptop, desktop, and phone in one place to share easily. This application is also good for office-to-home and on-the-road sharing of your important documents. Up to two gigabytes of storage is available for free, with more space available by subscription.

School Benefits

- Create new folders and updates directly on this website.
- Don't have to e-mail files to yourself anymore.
- Have a district drop box and share files between administrators.

Weebly for Education

http://education.weebly.com

Create a free website or blog in minutes by using a simple drag-and-drop interface. There are no advertisements. This is one of *Time*'s 50 Best websites of the Year. Students can build sites too.

School Benefit

- Manage your students' accounts.
- Accept homework assignments online.

- Keep your students and parents up to date.

SchoolRack

http://www.schoolrack.com

This is an easy-to-use website that lets you create a free classroom or educational blog to keep students, parents, and others informed outside of class.

School Benefits

- Share information, documents, and files.

- Hold discussions online or outside of class.

- Report grades online to students or their parents.

- Keep in touch with private messaging.

SchoolNotes

http://new.schoolnotes.com

This is a great school-to-home communication tool that lets teachers and students unite. Teachers can post information, homework, and other class information on their own personal page for parents to access. This is a free service.

School Benefits

- Books recommended for teachers and parents.

- Today's column pertaining to education.

- Showcase Teacher of the Month.

- Classroom management tip of the day.

- Teacher tool of the day.

ClassTools.net

http://www.classtools.net

Create free educational games, quizzes, activities, and diagrams in seconds. Host them on your own blog, website, or intranet.

School Benefits

- A lot of resources in one location.

- No passwords are necessary

- Ability to host your creations on your own website or school blog.

Resources

The forms and agendas found in this section may be reproduced in their entirety for one building's educational staff. If the forms and agendas need to be used in multiple buildings or districts, please contact the author for written permission.

Administrative Professional Development Planning Form

Use this form to create your own year-long professional development plan. Fill in the form below with the instructional E-Tools that you have found most interesting. Add any management E-Tools that you feel your staff would use. Be careful in selecting your tools to share. You don't want to overwhelm your staff if there are many digital novices. Maybe choosing one challenging E-Tool and one less difficult E-Tool will help your staff ease into the world of technology.

Day 1

Time Frame: Choose one below

Year Start   Sept   Oct   Nov   Dec   Jan   Feb   Mar   Apr   May   Year End

Agenda:

Half-day (4 hour) Agenda   Full-day (8 hour) Agenda   E-ProDev Agenda

E-Tool(s):

Choice 1:_____ Choice 2:_____

Administrative Tech Tool 1:_____

Administrative Tech Tool 2:_____

Day 2

Time Frame: Choose one below

Year Start   Sept   Oct   Nov   Dec   Jan   Feb   Mar   Apr   May   Year End

Agenda:

Half-day (4 hour) Agenda   Full-day (8 hour) Agenda   E-ProDev Agenda

E-Tool(s):

Choice 1:_____ Choice 2:_____

Administrative Tech Tool 1:_____

Administrative Tech Tool 2:_____

Day 3

Time Frame: Choose one below

Year Start   Sept   Oct   Nov   Dec   Jan   Feb   Mar   Apr   May   Year End

Agenda:

  Half-day (4 hour) Agenda   Full-day (8 hour) Agenda   E-ProDev Agenda

E-Tool(s):

Choice 1:_____ Choice 2:_____

Administrative Tech Tool 1:_____

Administrative Tech Tool 2:_____

Day 4

Time Frame: Choose one below

Year Start   Sept   Oct   Nov   Dec   Jan   Feb   Mar   Apr   May   Year End

Agenda:

  Half-day (4 hour) Agenda   Full-day (8 hour) Agenda   E-ProDev Agenda

E-Tool(s):

Choice 1:_____ Choice 2:_____

Administrative Tech Tool 1:_____

Administrative Tech Tool 2:_____

Day 5

Time Frame: Choose one below

Year Start   Sept   Oct   Nov   Dec   Jan   Feb   Mar   Apr   May   Year End

Agenda:

  Half-day (4 hour) Agenda   Full-day (8 hour) Agenda   E-ProDev Agenda

E-Tool(s):

Choice 1:_____ Choice 2:_____

Administrative Tech Tool 1:_____

Administrative Tech Tool 2:_____

Day 6

Time Frame: Choose one below

Year Start　　Sept　Oct　Nov　Dec　Jan　Feb　Mar　Apr　May　Year End

Agenda:

　Half-day (4 hour) Agenda　　　Full-day (8 hour) Agenda　　　E-ProDev Agenda

E-Tool(s):

Choice 1:_____ Choice 2:_____

Administrative Tech Tool 1:_____

Administrative Tech Tool 2:_____

Day 7

Time Frame: Choose one below

Year Start　　Sept　Oct　Nov　Dec　Jan　Feb　Mar　Apr　May　Year End

Agenda:

　Half-day (4 hour) Agenda　　　Full-day (8 hour) Agenda　　　E-ProDev Agenda

E-Tool(s):

Choice 1:_____ Choice 2:_____

Administrative Tech Tool 1:_____

Administrative Tech Tool 2:_____

Day 8

Time Frame: Choose one below

Year Start　　Sept　Oct　Nov　Dec　Jan　Feb　Mar　Apr　May　Year End

Agenda:

　Half-day (4 hour) Agenda　　　Full-day (8 hour) Agenda　　　E-ProDev Agenda

E-Tool(s):

Choice 1:_____ Choice 2:_____

Administrative Tech Tool 1:_____

Administrative Tech Tool 2:_____

Day 9

Time Frame: Choose one below

Year Start   Sept   Oct   Nov   Dec   Jan   Feb   Mar   Apr   May   Year End

Agenda:

Half-day (4 hour) Agenda   Full-day (8 hour) Agenda   E-ProDev Agenda

E-Tool(s):

Choice 1:_____ Choice 2:_____

Administrative Tech Tool 1:_____

Administrative Tech Tool 2:_____

Day 10

Time Frame: Choose one below

Year Start   Sept   Oct   Nov   Dec   Jan   Feb   Mar   Apr   May   Year End

Agenda:

Half-day (4 hour) Agenda   Full-day (8 hour) Agenda   E-ProDev Agenda

E-Tool(s):

Choice 1:_____ Choice 2:_____

Administrative Tech Tool 1:_____

Administrative Tech Tool 2:_____

Once you have completed the planning form, you can begin to modify the next form, which is a welcome letter to the staff outlining your newly created professional development plan. Consider adding this to a beginning-of-the-year letter sent to your staff during the first few days of school.

Beginning of the Year Welcome Letter

To: Faculty and Staff

From:_____

Date:_____

Re: Beginning-of-the-Year Professional Development Plan

    Welcome back to yet another exciting year. This is the outline of the plan for our professional development days. Our theme for this year will be Instructional Technology Tools. This will be an exceptional year with many opportunities to use some of the more proven instructional E-Tools for the classroom. I hope that you are as excited about the prospect of learning new and interesting ways to engage our students in their learning as I am to share these E-Tools with you.

Once the teachers are aware of the yearly plan, your next step will be to prepare the agenda for the first professional development day. The next form is a preplanned agenda. Modify this agenda to fit your time restraints and choose the instructional and managerial E-Tools your staff will learn.

Reproducible Full-day Agenda

To: Faculty and Staff

From:_____

Date_____

Re: Professional Development Full-day Agenda

　　Below you will find the agenda for our professional development day. Please adhere to the schedule as closely as possible. It will be a full day with a lot of exciting and creative opportunities.

Time:_____:　　　Introduction

Time:_____:　　　How to use the E-Tool (Title_____)

Time:_____:　　　Quick Start Guide

Time:_____:　　　Exit Card and Break

Time:_____:　　　Response to Exit Cards

Time:_____:　　　Creative Time

Time:_____:　　　Lunch

Time:_____:　　　Show, Share and Discuss

Time:_____:　　　Break time

Time:_____:　　　Collaborate, Organize, Research, and Communicate

　　　　　　　　　　Title 1_____ Title 2_____

Time:_____:　　　Exit Card and Evaluation

These are the three questions that need to be answered on each exit card indicated on the agenda:

- What new thing did I learn today?

- How am I first going to use this new instructional E-Tool?

- What questions or concerns do I still need to have addressed?

This will be a great experience, and I hope that everyone learns as much as I did investigating these instructional E-Tools.

Sincerely, _____

Reproducible Half-day Agenda

To: Faculty and Staff

From:_____

Date_____

Re: Professional Development Half-day Agenda

   Below you will find the agenda for our professional development day. Please adhere to the schedule as closely as possible. It will be a half day with a lot of exciting and creative opportunities.

This professional development session will be held in the AM/PM (please circle one).

Time:_____: Introduction

Time:_____: How to use the E-Tool (Title_____)

Time:_____: Quick Start Guide

Time:_____: Exit Card and Break

Time:_____: Creative Time

Time:_____: Show, Share and Discuss

Time:_____: Collaborate, Organize, Research and Communicate
                        Title 1_____Title 2_____

Time:_____: Exit Card and Evaluation

These are the three questions that need to be answered on each exit card indicated on the agenda:

- What new thing did I learn today?

- How am I first going to use this new instructional E-Tool?

- What questions or concerns do I still need to have addressed?

This will be a great experience, and I hope that everyone learns as much as I did investigating this instructional E-Tool.

Sincerely, _____

Reproducible E-ProDev Day Packet

To: Faculty and Staff

From:_____

Date_____

Re: E-Professional Development Day Packet

Below you will find the agenda and packet for our E-ProDev day. Please adhere to the schedule as closely as possible. It will be a full day with a lot of exciting and creative opportunities. Please follow this packet specifically and turn in all materials to the proper location.

The E-Tools for this E-ProDev day are:

Instructional Tool 1:_____

Instructional Tool 2:_____

Management Tool 1:_____

Management Tool 2:_____

Turn in all electronic documentation to http://www._____

And/or e-mail documentation to:_____

The E-ProDev website is available to you to see examples of various projects as well as providing a place to store your project URL. On the E-ProDev website (http://www.furmanr.com) you will see a menu and a tab named E-ProDev. You will use several of the menu tabs for various parts of the E-ProDev day. This packet will guide you through the website and each menu tab that will be used to find the necessary information to complete the day's projects.

The day is broken down by minutes so that you can finish the projects in a time frame equivalent to one school day. All answers to the project questions should first be typed into a word processing document and then transferred to the e-mail address/website URL written above for verification that the activities have been completed.

Time Frame and Activities

Anticipatory Set (30 min.)

Answer the following brainstorming questions regarding technology:

1. What types of instructional technology do you currently use in your classroom?

2. What are your classroom goals or class mission statement?

3. What technology do you think could help you to achieve your mission?

4. In what ways do you think technology would not be helpful in achieving your mission?

5. In what ways do you think technology can be used as a tool for students to learn, rather than just as a presentation tool?

Procedures 1 (30 min.)

Go to http://www.furmanr.com and click the forum tab in the menu. Review the example for E-Tool 1 that was chosen by your district. The name of the E-Tool will be found at the top of the form given to you by your district. Read through the tutorial in this packet and then answer the following questions:

1. How do you see this instructional E-Tool being used in your classroom?

2. What do you see as the roadblocks to using this technology?

3. How can we remove these barriers so that you can use this technology?

4. What do you think you need to learn to be able to use this technology?

Guided Practice (30 min.)

Preplan a lesson in which you will use the E-Tool. Answer the following questions:

1. What are the goals for the lesson?

2. What is the essential question you want the class to be able to answer by the end of the lesson?

3. What type of technology would be useful for this type of lesson or objective? Why?

4. What are the benefits of using this E-Tool as compared to traditional teaching methods?

5. What will the students be creating using this technology?

6. Write a detailed plan outlining what you/your students wish to create using this technology. (If the outcome is a student project, the teacher will create an example.)

Independent Practice (100 min.)

Review the tutorial in your packet that corresponds with the first E-Tool your administrator has assigned. Using the E-Tool, create a project that you will use in your lesson. If this is an example to be used with your students, make sure it is complete and follows all of the rules that you expect your students to follow. If this is a tutorial for your students, then make sure it is simple enough for your students to completely understand as they work through it independently. Upload the finished product (or a URL to the finished product) to http://www.furmanr.com and/or the location chosen by your district.

Procedures Part 2 (30 min.)

Review the example of E-Tool 2 listed on http://www.furmanr.com. Read though the tutorial in this packet. Answer the following questions:

1. How do you see this instructional E-Tool being used in your classroom?

2. What do you see as the roadblocks to using this technology?

3. How can we remove these barriers so that you can use this technology?

4. What do you think you need to learn to be able to use this technology?

Guided Practice (30 min.)

Preplan a second lesson in which you will use this E-Tool. Answer the following questions:

1. What are the goals for the lesson?

2. What is the essential question you want the class to be able to answer by the end of the lesson?

3. What type of technology would be useful for this type of lesson or objective? Why?

4. What are the benefits of using this E-Tool as compared to traditional teaching methods?

5. What will the students be creating using this technology?

6. Write a detailed plan outlining what you/your students wish to create using this technology. (If the outcome is a student project the teacher will create an example.)

Independent Practice (100 min.)

Review the tutorial in your packet that corresponds with the second E-Tool your administrator has assigned. Using the E-Tool, create a project that you will use in your lesson. If this is an example to be used with your students, make sure it is complete and follows all of the rules that you expect your students to follow. If this is a tutorial for your students, then make sure it is simple enough for your students to completely understand as they work through it independently. Upload the finished product (or a URL to the finished product) to http://www.furmanr.com and/or the location chosen by your district.

Exploration (40 min.)

Go to the tab named links on the http://www.furmanr.com website and find the two tools for which you have submitted your exercises. Answer the following questions with regard to both E-Tools.

1. What do you see as the benefit of this E-Tool?

2. How would this E-Tool help you with your job?

3. What are some creative ways you could see this E-Tool being used:

    a. In the classroom?

    b. In the community?

    c. With parents?

    d. With fellow teachers?

    a. Other?

Once you have finished all of the assigned activities, you must:

1. Upload the URL of your project or the project file itself to http://www.furmanr.com in the forum section under district verifications

2. Copy and paste the answers to the activity questions to the Forum section of the E-ProDev web site under district verifications wwww.furmanr.com and/or the location chosen by your district. Add it as a post and include your name, school name, and grade taught.

3. Send any other pertinent information to the location chosen by your district.

Congratulations! You have completed the E-ProDev day. The final form you must complete is the evaluation form. This form will help to your district to modify and enhance the next E-ProDev day. Your feedback is always of great importance in improving the integrity of this program.

Evaluation Form for Professional Development Day

Name_____ Date_____ Grade_____

Half-day or Full-day or E-ProDev (Please circle one)

E-Tools that were taught:_____

Please respond to the evaluation questions below so that we may improve the next professional development day. Please circle a number from 1 to 5, with 5 being the best.

This session was a good source of useful information.	1	2	3	4	5
The E-Tools that were taught in this session will be useful in the classroom.	1	2	3	4	5
The session was organized and time efficient.	1	2	3	4	5
I can see myself using these E-Tools.	1	2	3	4	5
The tutorials were effective and useful.	1	2	3	4	5
I am looking forward to the next session so that I can learn more E-Tools.	1	2	3	4	5

Comments or Suggestions:

_____

_____

_____

_____

_____

_____

Technology Project Rubric

Category	Advanced	Proficient	Basic	Below Basic
Content Quality and Accuracy	Project content is accurate and uses at least three supporting details. All facts relate to the topic.	Project content is accurate and uses 1-2 supporting details. Most facts relate to the topic.	Project content is accurate but there are no supporting details. Facts do not relate to the topic.	Project content is not accurate.
Writing and Grammar	There are no grammatical errors and no spelling errors.	There are no grammatical errors, but there may be 1–2 spelling errors.	There are 1–2 grammatical errors and several spelling errors.	There are many grammatical and spelling errors.
Organization and Layout	Presentation has a strong design. The viewer understands what he/she is to gain from this project.	Presentation has a strong design. The viewer may be confused about project intent.	Presentation is difficult to follow. Viewer may be confused.	No thought seems to have been given to the design of the project.
Sources	All sources, including images, video, and documents, are correctly cited in an acceptable format.	Most sources, including images, video, and documents, are correctly cited in an acceptable format.	Sources are cited but not in an acceptable format.	Sources are not cited.
Graphics and/ or Enhancements	Images and enhancements are used nicely to add to the content of the project.	Images and enhancements are used well but may be overshadowing content.	Images and enhancements overshadow the content, or there are too few enhancements.	No enhancements.

This rubric can be used to fairly "grade" a project created by your professional development participants. This will ensure equity when preparing to discuss the final electronic project and to give suggestions for improvement.

Works Cited

American Association of School Librarians. "AASL Standards for the 21st Century Learner." *American Association of School Librarians*. American Library Association, 2007. Web. 11 January 2012.

Armstrong, Thomas. Honoring Diversity in Human Growth and Learning: Multiple Intelligence. (www.thomasarmstrong.com/multiple_intelligences.php). Thomas Armstrong, 2011. Web. 11 January 2012.

Bacon, Francis. Henry G.Bohn. *The Works of Lord Bacon: Philosophical Works*. Vol.1. Bungay: John Childs & Son, 1854. P.280. The Library of the University of California, 25 January 2008. Web. 16 January 2012.

Beaver, Robin and Jean Moore. Learning and Leading with Technology. *Curriculum Design And Technology Integration: A Model To Use Technology In Support Of Knowledge Generation And Higher-Order Thinking Skills*. 2.1 (2004): 11 January 2012.

Bloom, Benjamin S. and David R. Krathwohl. *Taxonomy of Educational Objectives: The Classification of Educational Goals*. New York: Longmans, 1956. Print.

"Good to Great: Why Some Companies Make the Leap … and Others Don't." *WikiSummaries*. WikiSummaries, 24 January 2008. Web. 14 January 2012.

Grunwald and Associates. "Educators, Technology and 21st Century Skills: Dispelling Five Myths." *Walden University*. Walden University, 2010. Web. 11 January 2012.

Hopkins, Gary. "Principals Offer Practical, Timely Time Management Tips." *Education World*. Education World, Inc., 2008. Web. 11 January 2012.

Ibarra, Herminia & Morten Hansen. "Are You a Collaborative Leader? Succeeding in a Hyper-Connected World." *Harvard Business Review*. Harvard Business Publishing, 11 March 2011. Web. 16 January 2012.

Khurana, Simran. "Andrew Carnegie Quotations." *About.com Guide*. New York Times Company, 2012. Web. 11 January 2012.

"Marcus Aurelius Quotes." *iPerceptive*. iPerceptive, 2011. Web. 16 January 2012.

E-Tools Cited

4shared.com 4shared.com. Web. June 2011. <http://www.4shared.com>.

BonzoBox. BonzoBox.com. Web. June 2011. <http://www.bonzobox.com>.

Bookr. Pimpampum. Web. Apr.–May 2011. <http://www.pimpampum.net/bookr>.

Bubbl.us. Bubbl.us. Web. May 2011. <https://bubbl.us/>.

ChartGizmo. ChartGizmo. Web. May 2011. <http://www.chartgizmo.com>.

classroom4teachers.org. classroom4teachers.org. Web. 9 May 2011. <http://www.classroom4teachers.org>.

ClassTools. Classtools.com. Web. May 2011. <http://www.classtools.com>.

DecideAlready. DecideAlready. Web. 1 Apr. 2011. <https://decidealready.com/>.

Diffen. Diffen. Web. May 2011. <http://www.diffen.com>.

Dropbox. Dropbox. Web. May–June 2011. <http://www.dropbox.com>.

DropSend. DropSend. Web. May–June 2011. <http://www.dropsend.com>.

eHow. Program documentation. *eHow. | eHow.com*. Web. May–June 2011. <http://www.ehow.com>.

Gliffy. Gliffy. Web. May–June 2011. <http://www.gliffy.com>.

Glogster. Glogster. Web. Mar.–Apr. 2011. <http://www.glogster.com>.

GoAnimate. GoAnimate. Web. Jan.–Feb. 2011. <http://www.goanimate.com>.

GoAnimate4Schools. GoAnimate for Schools and Educators. Web. June–July 2011. <http://goanimate4schools.com/public_index>.

Google Calendar. Google Calendar. Web. May–June 2011. <http://calendar.google.com>.

Google Docs. Google Docs. Web. May–June 2011. <http://docs.google.com>.

Guerilla Mail. Guerilla Mail. Web. Mar.–Apr. 2011. <http://www.guerrillamail.com/>.

HassleMe. HassleMe. Web. Mar.–Apr. 2011. <http://www.hassleme.co.uk>.

HitMeLater. *HitMeLater*. Web. Apr.–May 2011. <http://hitmelater.com>.

Hot Potatoes. *Hot Potatoes*. Web. Feb.–Mar. 2011. <http://www.hotpot.uvic.ca>.

Infoencrypt. Computer software. *Infoencrypt*. Web. Apr.–May 2011. <http://www.infoencrypt. com>.

Infoplease. *Infoplease*. Web. Mar.–Apr. 2011. <http://www.infoplease.com>.

JustPaste.it. *JustPaste.it*. Web. Apr.–May 2011. <http://www.justpaste.it>.

KeePass. *KeePass*. Web. Mar.–Apr. 2011. <http://keepass.info/>.

Launchy. *Launchy*. Web. Mar.–Apr. 2011. <http://www.launchy.net/>.

Masher. *Masher*. Web. May–June 2011. <http://www.masher.com>.

Meetsee. *Meetsee*. Web. Mar.–Apr. 2011. <http://meetsee.com/>.

Museum Box. *Museum Box*. Web. Sept.–Oct. 2011. <http://www.museumbox.com>.

Only2Clicks. *Only2Clicks*. Web. Apr.–May 2011. <http://www.only2clicks.com>.

ooVoo. *ooVoo*. Web. Apr.–May 2011. <http://www.oovoo.com>.

Pandora Recovery. *Pandora File Recovery*. Web. Apr.–May 2011. <http://www.pandorarecovery. com>.

Paper Critters. *Paper Critters*. Web. Mar.–Apr. 2011. <http://www.papercritters.com>.

pdfforge.org. *pdfforge.org*. Web. Mar.–Apr. 2011. <http://www.pdfforge.org>.

Penzu. *Penzu*. Web. Apr.–May 2011. <http://www.penzu.com>.

PictureTrail. *PictureTrail*. Web. May–June 2011. <http://www.picturetrail.com>.

Policy Tool. *Policy Tool*. Web. Apr.–May 2011. <http://www.policytool.com>.

Poll Everywhere. *Poll Everywhere*. Web. Apr.–May 2011. <http://www.polleverywhere.com>.

Premier Survey. *Premier Survey*. Web. Apr.–May 2011. <http://www.premiersurvey.com>.

Prezi. *Prezi*. Web. Mar.–Apr. 2011. <http://prezi.com>.

quikmaps. *quikmaps*. Web. Apr.–May 2011. <http://quikmaps.com/>.

SAM Animation. *SAM Animation*. Web. Mar.–Apr. 2011. <http://www.samanimation.com>.

SchoolNotes. *SchoolNotes*. Web. Apr.–May 2011. <http://www.schoolnotes.com>.

SchoolRack. *SchoolRack*. Web. Feb.–Mar. 2011. <http://www.schoolrack.com/>.

Scratch. *Scratch*. Web. May–June 2011. <http://www.scratch.mit.edu>.

Sharendipity. *Sharendipity*. Web. May–June 2011. <http://www.sharendipity.com>.

Solvr. *Solvr*. Web. Mar.–Apr. 2011. <http://www.a.freshbrain.com/solvr/>.

Spruz. *Spruz*. Web. Apr.–May 2011. <http://www.spruz.com>.

stickybits. <http://www.stickybits.com/>

TargetMap. TargetMap. Web. Mar.–Apr. 2011. <http://www.targetmap.com>.

VoiceThread. VoiceThread. Web. 09 July 2011. <http://www.voicethread.com>.

VUVOX. VUVOX. Web. Mar.–Apr. 2011. <http://www.vuvox.com>.

WebQuest. WebQuest. Web. Feb.–Mar. 2011. <http://webquest.org/index.php>.

Webs. Webs. Web. Mar.–Apr. 2011. <http://www.webs.com>.

Webspiration. Webspiration. Web. Apr.–May 2011. <http://www.inspiration.com>.

Weebly for Education. Weebly. Web. Mar.–Apr. 2011. <http://education.weebly.com/>.

WizIQ. WizIQ. Web. Apr.–May 2011. <http://www.wiziq.com>.

Zoho Creator. Zoho. Web. Apr.–May 2011. <http://www.zoho.com/creator>.

Zunal. Zunal. Web. Apr.–May 2011. <http://www.zunal.com>.

Additional Resources

Forehand, Mary. "Bloom's Taxonomy." *Emerging Perspectives on Learning, Teaching, and Technology.* Ed. M. Orey. Athens, GA: University of Georgia, 2005. N. pag. 19 April 2010. Web. 11 January 2012.

Gardner, Howard. *Frames of Mind: The Theory of Multiple Intelligences.* New York: Basic, 1983. Print.